faith can give us WINGS

THE ART OF LETTING GO

Notker Wolf

*Translated from German
by Mark S. Burrows and Ute S. Molitor*

PARACLETE PRESS
BREWSTER, MASSACHUSETTS

2013 First Printing

Faith Can Give Us Wings: The Art of Letting Go

English Translation Copyright © 2013 by Mark S. Burrows and Ute S. Molitor

Original title: Schmetterlinge im Bauch, Warum der Glaube Flugel verleigt by Abtprimas Notker Wolf © 2011 by adeo Verlag in der Gerth Medien GmbH, Asslar, a division of Verlagsgruppe Random House GmbH, Munchen, Germany.

ISBN 978-1-61261-303-1

Library of Congress Cataloging-in-Publication Data is available.
ISBN 978-1-61261-303-1

10 9 8 7 6 5 4 3 2 1

Published by Paraclete Press
Brewster, Massachusetts
www.paracletepress.com
Printed in the United States of America

CONTENTS

why have faith?

Firm Ground Beneath Our Feet

"Why do you look so happy?"

A woman asked me this question during her visit to Rome, and it prompted me to write this book. I hear this question more and more often in interactions with others. Who among us doesn't want to lead a happy life? It takes a person with vitality and curiosity to ask such a question, one who is willing to be transparent about her search and open to the response of others.

The question about happiness is far too important to answer with a quick platitude. What does it mean to find joy in life? What grounds me? What would you say if you were asked such questions? What is the foundation of your life?

In many respects, I realize that my life as a monk is quite different from yours. But we do share many of the same wishes, longings, and questions.

My answers grow out of my life experiences. They bestow me—this much I am able to reveal—with a great inner freedom.

Does it surprise you to hear that a monk, whose life seems to be bound by a strict set of rules, feels free? Perhaps you're even more surprised to hear me suggest that many of my experiences resemble your own. This is why I want to talk about them.

A Foundation That Sets Us Free

Those who remain full of questions are willing to take a hard look at their lives, examining both the beautiful and not so beautiful aspects of their experiences. Some may interpret this as weakness, especially those who think they have all the answers, but I don't agree. I regard seekers as strong people because they sense that life has a greater purpose than what they know, one that is always waiting to be discovered. Seekers are people in motion who will not be satisfied with premature answers because they want to come home to themselves. They do not deny the fragmentation they experience in their lives and in our world but are willing to face it on their own journey.

Where do you stand right now? Have you found your place in life, or do you feel that some changes are needed? If so, what can help to guide you?

My answers come as a witness to my own faith, but I am not always sure that my view of life will be understood. Why is this so? Because I sense that faith, at least as we often speak of it, has increasingly become a point of division. Some would like to believe but find themselves struggling with doubt and falling into despair because of the difficult questions they face or the disappointing experiences they've had in church. For others, the Christian faith has become irrelevant. When we read about religious issues, the topics are often controversial, such as pedophilia scandals, the pill, condoms, or the celibacy of priests.

These controversies are not my concern because I intend to tell you of the beauty, comfort, and joy that is ours because of our faith as Christians.

Joy, comfort, beauty: do we generally associate these words with Christian faith? If so, let us share our experiences. If these realities are not what you usually associate with believing, I would be delighted if you'd be willing to entertain the thought that there might be another side to the question. I share this in the hope that I can win you over in this journey of exploration and discovery.

Through my work as Abbot Primate of the Benedictines, I travel the world and am often deeply touched by the depth of joy and trust in God that I encounter among people. I see how faith is shaped by what I imagine to be mosaic stones. Entrusted to us in childhood, these pieces on the ground represent a foundation of our experiences, and yet they are part of a larger work that includes prayer and music, witness and community. This great mosaic is painted with the colors of hope, welcome, and care— pieces that many of us have yet to discover.

Do you remember the first time you fell in love?

You probably didn't know what the experience would feel like before it happened. Maybe you experienced the sensation of butterflies fluttering in your stomach. Did you think incessantly of your beloved? Did your knees tremble when you saw your dearest, as if the world suddenly shifted from black and white to color? Finding faith can be much the same. Imagine that your experiences thus far reflect only part of what characterizes life with God. Imagine an entire world yet to be discovered—one that is greater, more vibrant, and more beautiful than what you've imagined.

I want to immerse you in the great and colorful mosaic of Christian faith. But we must realize that this is a journey we take one step at a time.

Why believe?

"Why should we believe at all?" This question will be our focus, together with the first—not only why I *look* so happy, but also why I actually *am* a happy person. Next I will share with you how I try to live out my faith on a daily basis and how you can do the same. My ordinary life ceases to be ordinary when I realize that God participates in shaping it and does not desire that

I remain unchanged. The Christian faith can evolve into a life perspective with the power to set us free.

Does the prospect that God wants to be involved in your life frighten you? I hope not. Seekers are courageous; they refuse to evade their doubts as they set sail for a new and more fulfilling life. They know that their ship will survive being tossed about by the storms that come. They stand tall like a strong tree in the broad landscape of their life. Even when the wind sways them, they stand upright thanks to deep roots.

Finally Getting There

What is behind the feeling that other people have more authority over my life than I do? We each undergo this experience. Perhaps we have a boss who is impossible to please or a partner whose expectations exert enormous pressure on us. Perhaps we feel restricted by the unspoken rules that exist within a circle of friends, the expectations of our neighbors, or the pressures we feel in a club or church. An Abbot Primate is an easy and clear target for a variety of such projections, particularly because my life does not fit the mold that many people imagine a monk to inhabit. Some people assume that my frequent travel and passion for playing the electric guitar do not correspond with my vocation, when in fact both are a part of my chosen life.

Nobody questions that my presence is needed at monastic assemblies on various continents, but many seem confused about the ways that I show my love toward others and the form of my spiritual practice. We are all caught up in our lives, trying to remember to breathe while striving to meet the many expectations that come our way. Why is this so?

We all have a deep longing within us to be accepted and loved.

This longing often drives us. Can we be honest with ourselves about our motivation, or do we feel the impulse to rationalize this statement?

"It's not true," you might find yourself saying. "I carry so much responsibility at the office that it's necessary for me to work so many hours." Or: "I'm making all these extracurricular activities available to my kids because I'm supposed to nurture their growth." Or: "What about my need to be involved in organizing the parish festival? We can't have community if we don't invest ourselves in it, and anyway I like baking cakes." Or: "I should stop by for a short visit with my neighbor. True, I really don't like her, but I need to go for the sake of being a good neighbor." Or: "My boss needs the evaluation completed by tomorrow morning, and I haven't gone shopping yet." Or: "After the children have gone to bed, I finally find the quiet I have been craving, but my partner has other ideas."

Don't get me wrong; the world needs people who don't just think about themselves but take responsibility for their families, their jobs, and the world around them. But this is only one side of the coin. The other side reveals our true motivation: we long for the affirmation we receive for investing ourselves in others' lives and work. We enjoy hearing from a boss who tells us that we are irreplaceable and appreciate the pastor who thanks us for serving refreshments at the festival. We interpret these affirmations as signs of our success.

The personal and societal drive of our culture is rooted in our endeavor for affirmation. We want to be recognized and feel that our lives have purpose. But is it working? I have my doubts.

Too many people feel empty, mental illness is on the rise, and burnout is an increasing reality in our pressure-driven world. Many of us are heading in the wrong direction and find ourselves stuck in a cul-de-sac where we finally recognize we can't continue this way.

The problem is that we want to achieve affirmation and love. We want to get it from outside ourselves.

As long as we chase after the affirmation of others, we will find ourselves complying with the conditions they set for us. Life according to the faster-higher-further principle has come to resemble life on a hamster wheel: the harder we run the faster the wheel turns, leaving us exhausted but getting us nowhere.

The Comparison Trap

Just as damaging is the way we constantly compare our lives to the lives of others. The extent to which we are caught in this trap directly aligns with our satisfaction in possessing what others don't have. The same is true in our dissatisfaction over the fact that others have access to possibilities closed to us.

But in reality, our deepest longing is to be loved, recognized, and accepted. We want this experience in a way that deepens our sense of freedom. Herein lies the first key to our question about joy.

The answer emerged for me during a visit by a group of Japanese Buddhist monastics to Rome. "Why are you Western monks so happy?" they asked. There is a simple answer to this question, though it may be difficult to comprehend.

At the root of our monastic lives is the realization that we are deeply loved by God. But this truth is not only for monastics; everyone can experience it. God's love does not waver and is never unfaithful.

These assertions ground me most deeply in my life, both as a monk and a Christian. God loves me and affirms me. I don't need to fear losing this love because God will always love me, even those parts of me that I don't particularly like and that may not be likeable.

Allow this to sink in for a moment. It takes no time to read this sentence; on a cognitive level it is easily understood. But take a moment and try to breathe it in. When we receive it within us, and begin to "listen" with what St. Benedict in his Preface to the Rule calls "the ears of the heart," a journey of transformation begins to happen. It is a love I cannot earn and cannot lose. For all who yearn to belong, this love offers a path—a spiritual way rooted in the realization that each of us is profoundly loved not for what we do but because of who we are. Inner freedom begins when I recognize this truth deep in my heart, a realization that frees me from the constant pressure of needing to prove myself to others and to myself. In this way, the search for my true identity can emerge from a great inner calm. "Who am I? Am I somebody?" The answer is yes because this God has called me by name. God's call not only gives us a sense of well-being in daily life, but also (in contrast to the promises of our consumption-driven culture) extends uniquely beyond death. A remarkable perspective indeed.

In other words, I can say yes to myself because another says yes to me. Coming to recognize this tenet in our lives offers the true heart of belonging.

We will not discover this truth if we continue making ourselves the measure of all things, defining ourselves solely by what we want. Such a posture may look superficially attractive, but it will inevitably prove itself fickle, disappointing, and exhausting beyond words.

A Love That Carries Us

Love and friendship between two people is a beautiful gift, yet if we define ourselves solely through the other, the inadequacy of this approach to life and love becomes obvious when our idea of love falls apart. In such cases, both the relationship and a part of ourselves dies—a dimension of our experience that supplied us with love, recognition, and affection.

The truth is that you and I are already beloved; our worth is not the sum of our accomplishments. We can set out to accept and experience this truth at any point in our lives.

In this context, I am repeatedly touched by the parable of the Prodigal Son, a story that describes the love of God in a unique and complex way.

Then Jesus said, "There was a man who had two sons. The younger of them said to his father, 'Father, give me the share of the property that will belong to me.' So he divided his property between them. A few days later the younger son gathered all he had and traveled to a distant country, and there he squandered his property in dissolute living. When he had spent everything, a severe famine took place throughout that country, and he began to be in need. So he went and hired himself out to one of the citizens of that country, who sent him to his fields to feed the pigs. He would gladly have filled himself with the pods that the pigs were eating; and no one gave him anything. But when he came to himself he said, 'How many of my father's hired hands have bread enough and to spare, but here I am dying of hunger! I will get up and go to my father, and I will say to him, 'Father, I have sinned against heaven and before you; I am no longer worthy to be called your son; treat me like one of your hired hands.' So he set off and went to his father. But while he was still far off, his father saw him and was filled with compassion; he ran and put his arms around him and kissed him. Then the son said to him, 'Father, I have sinned against heaven and before you; I am no longer worthy to be called your son.' But the father said to his slaves, 'Quickly, bring out a robe—the best one—and put it on him; put a ring on his finger and sandals on his feet. And get the fatted calf and kill it, and let us eat and celebrate; for this son of

*mine was dead and is alive again; he was lost and is found!' And
they began to celebrate.*

"*Now his elder son was in the field; and when he came and
approached the house, he heard music and dancing. He called
one of the slaves and asked what was going on. He replied, 'Your
brother has come, and your father has killed the fatted calf,
because he has got him back safe and sound.' Then he became
angry and refused to go in. His father came out and began to
plead with him. But he answered his father, 'Listen! For all these
years I have been working like a slave for you, and I have never
disobeyed your command; yet you have never given me even a
young goat so that I might celebrate with my friends. But when
this son of yours came back, who has devoured your property
with prostitutes, you killed the fatted calf for him!' Then the
father said to him, 'Son, you are always with me, and all that is
mine is yours. But we had to celebrate and rejoice, because this
brother of yours was dead and has come to life; he was lost and
has been found.'*" (Lk. 15:11–32)

The father allows his son to leave. He gives him the freedom
to go his own way and experience life. Instead of following him
and forcing him to return, the father gives him his inheritance and
freedom to act on his own. Then the father waits. He waits for his
son to turn, even from a very great distance.

Rembrandt completed a beautiful and startlingly perceptive
painting of this story. Upon the son's return, we see the father
reaching around and placing his hands lovingly on his son's back;
his son rests his head gently against his father. In a similar ges-
ture of childlike trust, we are invited to turn in this way toward
God, who is glad to give us this freedom! We set out to make
our own experiences, but when we wander astray and desire to

return home, he will receive us with open arms like the father in Rembrandt's painting.

We are allowed to feel welcome and lean against God with trust. Our life circumstances will not improve immediately, but we don't walk the path alone.

Acceptance is the greatest gift of our lives, but are we aware of it? Though an affinity for this perspective remains, its breadth, radical nature, and freeing power are often not understood.

Imagine a situation in which you may not be accepted. In such circumstances, we often turn both the small and large lies of our lives into parachutes of escape. Our success at work is governed by our position in relation to others and not our real situation as a person. Likewise, when an intimate relationship becomes a routine lacking intimate recognition, we find ourselves tempted to change partners in our search for a new source of affirmation. In such a predicament, we find ourselves constantly on the lookout for new sources of intimacy that will give us a higher yield—deeper acceptance and more trustworthy affirmation.

Free at Last

I am convinced that only when we have truly understood our unconditional acceptance can we let go of these unhealthy desires.

When this reality takes root, we can set out on the exciting journey home to our true self without being afraid of what we might encounter. We can discover the unique person the creator planned and willed so carefully for us to be. We no longer need to function according to others' rules or modes of affirmation but can rely instead on the belief that we are sustained by God in all our being and doing, that we are accepted and find our deepest grounding in God's love.

This freedom allows us to make mistakes, take detours, fall down, and get up again—just like the prodigal son—in our journey home. God looks upon our failures like the father in Jesus's parable, accepting us in the midst of our mistakes and regardless of what we've hidden from others; he looks upon us not with judgment but with love. We find ourselves seen, as described so wonderfully in Psalm 139, in a way that lets us feel truly and completely loved.

This realization is what makes a life lived in freedom possible. It's a life we experience with butterflies in the stomach, one that we come to know with the kind of faith that gives us wings.

O LORD, you have searched me and known me.
You know when I sit down and when I rise up;
*   you discern my thoughts from far away.*
You search out my path and my lying down,
*   and are acquainted with all my ways.*
Even before a word is on my tongue,
*   O LORD, you know it completely.*
You hem me in, behind and before,
*   and lay your hand upon me.*
Such knowledge is too wonderful for me;
*   it is so high that I cannot attain it.*

Where can I go from your spirit?
*   Or where can I flee from your presence?*
If I ascend to heaven, you are there;
*   if I make my bed in Sheol, you are there.*
If I take the wings of the morning
*   and settle at the farthest limits of the sea,*

even there your hand shall lead me,
  and your right hand shall hold me fast.
If I say, "Surely the darkness shall cover me,
  and the light around me become night,"
even the darkness is not dark to you;
  the night is as bright as the day,
  for darkness is as light to you.

For it was you who formed my inward parts;
  you knit me together in my mother's womb.
I praise you, for I am fearfully and wonderfully made.
  Wonderful are your works;
that I know very well.
  My frame was not hidden from you,
when I was being made in secret,
  intricately woven in the depths of the earth.
Your eyes beheld my unformed substance.
In your book were written
  all the days that were formed for me,
  when none of them as yet existed.
How weighty to me are your thoughts, O God!
  How vast is the sum of them!
I try to count them—they are more than the sand;
  I come to the end—I am still with you. (Ps. 139:1–18)

Recognizing Who We Are

What we are concerned with is the matter of our identity, the question of *who we are* at the deepest core of our being. Though this has not always been the case, the question of identity has become more urgent. In the past, more people were immersed in communities, both large and small; they seldom considered themselves to be the center of attention, especially within the family unit. Everyone had their place and identity, whether it be as father, grandfather, grandmother, mother, or child. But today many people feel alone, as if living on a remote island.

Given the isolation many experience today (forty-seven to fifty-two percent of the people surveyed living in urban households are single), it's only natural that questions about identity are voiced more frequently: "Who am I, really? What is the source of my true self?"

We are searching for ourselves, but too often we travel down a dead-end road.

We have a great yearning for self-discovery but too often find ourselves absorbed in a search for external recognition and approval. We wear our medals and titles so that everyone can see how important we are. Many professionals—doctors, lawyers, professors, and the like—are indignant when they think they are not being regarded with the esteem they deserve. I notice this issue when people ask how they should address me. My title is irrelevant; it does not make me a better or worse human being.

I am convinced that as human beings we cannot derive our identity from within us. Our worth proceeds from God's creation and affirmation of us. This reality gives us confidence and sets us free.

Such faith allows us to see that we don't have to be important or powerful. We no longer need as much external approval. This new awareness allows us to take a healthy step back and look at ourselves. For example, I am often asked how I feel, but I can't and don't want to answer this question without sensing God's loving gaze upon me. Why? Because the way I feel in the moment is put in perspective when I am aware of his love. I believe this *being with* God constitutes the heart of Christian faith. It creates a primal trust that grounds our identity. By faith we come to know ourselves as the beloved of God.

Moreover, our identity as God's beloved impacts how we view others. If God loves us, he equally loves our neighbor—even the ones we may not like. When we begin to recognize this, we find ourselves learning to ask a new question: "How will I regard and treat this person who is loved by God as much as I am?" This revelation creates an opening in the sphere of human interaction, making it possible to relate to others in a new way.

It's Not All About Me!

Self-discovery is a deeply personal matter, but it should not lead us to become frantic. While many among us may avoid the question of identity, our evasion does not make the matter any less important. Though it may sound old-fashioned, what ultimately matters is our covenantal relationship with God, whether we have experienced it or not. Our journey toward this realization begins by opening our clenched hands so that another can take hold of them. This *other* can be God, but

God often draws near to us through our relationships. We first discover ourselves through an *I–Thou* relationship, to borrow a term from Martin Buber. The human person is a relational, and thus dialogical, being.

Other claims can be made, but no one has yet shown me another approach for true happiness. In the practice of Buddhism, we can insulate ourselves from others, immersing ourselves in Zen meditation and learning to concentrate on the rhythm of our breath. While this discipline can free us from our surroundings and perhaps from our desires, I wonder if it brings true joy in the way that *being-with* our fellow human beings does.

Finding True Joy

True joy can only be found with God. Yet the world incessantly tells us: "You need a new house; you need a great car! You need those elegant shoes and that tailored suit!" Even though possessing things can make us feel alive, we know how quickly this feeling disappears.

How can we begin to be attracted to the kind of life in which less means more, despite the fact that the world disagrees?

Perhaps we need to reframe the question. This journey is about *your* joy and the question of what brings *you* deep gladness beyond the delights of everyday life.

We cannot approach this question in a purely intellectual sense. How, then, do we proceed? Let me begin by telling you how I do it.

When I sit in my office in Rome, I immediately notice, and often try to ignore, its cluttered state. Mountains of magazines, books, and essays surround me. Though I am always pleased to recycle what paper I can, I don't recognize my need to get rid of the piles until they are gone. Those things that seemed so important turned out to be nonessential.

In our search for joy we must learn to recognize that we don't need everything we think we do. Consider the success of books marketed to simplify our lives. "Purge yourself of everything!" they proclaim, thereby helping us to engage in a kind of permanent fast—one of the most misunderstood yet helpful of Christian practices.

We don't need Lent to torture and punish ourselves. What matters is the recovery and preservation of our inner freedom. We will feel much lighter and even liberated. As the title of this book points out, we need to learn how to fly—a task much easier for a seagull than a turkey.

We will explore the themes of true joy, simplicity, and fasting later in the book. At this point, I would like Scripture to speak. In Paul's First Letter to Timothy, we hear the summons to moderation:

Of course, there is great gain in godliness combined with contentment; for we brought nothing into the world, so that we can take nothing out of it; but if we have food and clothing, we will be content with these. But those who want to be rich fall into temptation and are trapped by many senseless and harmful desires that plunge people into ruin and destruction. For the love of money is a root of all kinds of evil, and in their eagerness to be rich some have wandered away from the faith and pierced themselves with many pains. (1 Tim. 6:6–10)

This text is very relevant for us today. Too often we think of godliness and contentment in life-denying terms, a cultural inheritance of Christian faith no longer relevant in our present-day search for happiness.

But consider the outcry of those who suffer because of the "harmful desires" of others. Again we recognize two sides to the coin. "Some have wandered away from the faith and pierced themselves with many pains," the apostle tells us. They hurt not only themselves, but others as well.

The recent financial crisis exposes the madness of our globally interconnected system. Underlying its impact is a personal dimension of suffering that can only be ignored by those whose lives are disconnected from the existential needs of others. In truth, this suffering is real for those who are poor both materially and spiritually.

As far as I'm concerned, all wounded and abandoned human beings whose love has been rejected are in personal danger. So are those who face mental exhaustion but can't find the courage to stop, consider their condition, and take charge of their lives.

Having the faith that gives us wings enables us to pause and take notice of what truly matters, a difficult task in today's consumer-driven culture. Each of us must come to terms with the life we've imagined for ourselves. Instead of thinking, *not possible is not acceptable*, we should tell ourselves that *going on like this is impossible*.

We cannot discover our true identity through the frantic accumulation of status symbols and success. Instead, we must find the way to orient ourselves toward God and other human beings.

Finding the Truth about My Life

The tendency to see the Christian faith as one worldview among many runs rampant in modern culture. But this heresy distorts the truth of what faith is: a relationship between God and myself; between God and my neighbor; and thus between my neighbor and myself. The interpersonal nature of these relationships is integral to true Christianity. Though this concept may seem strange in our day, we must remember that we have embarked on an exploratory journey that gives credence to the experiences of others, even if we don't see them on the daily news or read about them in the paper. Our image of faith is always tied to the way we experience it.

Let me share an illustration. If I have always been served overcooked steak, I come to believe that steak will always taste dry and tough. Once I get to enjoy a perfectly cooked steak, however, my attitude suddenly changes!

What matters is our openness toward perspectives we have not experienced, which requires setting certain prejudices aside. For example, when I look beyond the confines of the Catholic tradition, I am profoundly touched by the evangelical emphasis on a personal relationship with God, and particularly with Jesus. I don't have to subscribe to the whole of evangelicals' theology in order to appreciate their recognition of the human need and desire to experience God. Many evangelicals live their faith in all aspects of their lives, not just on Sunday morning. Their congregations have established authentic fellowship practices in the same way that many Catholic and mainline Protestant congregations do, giving God a central role in their lives.

Even if our experiences of faith and the church have been entirely positive, this fundamental point remains: faith leads us to the core of our being because it encourages us to walk our path with honesty and truth—toward ourselves, toward God, and toward our fellow human beings. Jesus spoke of the threefold harmony of this faithful and authentic path: "I am the way, and the truth, and the life" (John 14:6). First, let's take a closer look at truth.

Truth and Truthfulness

What does it mean to live with great truthfulness toward God and our fellow human beings? This question reveals to me the ways in which I can betray others. I can pretend about my faith to the point that I fool myself. But when I kneel in front of the tabernacle in church and know that God is present there, it is clear to me that I can't fool the God who made me and knows me. In this way God frees me of my illusions.

Though I may not see the entire truth about myself, I no longer consciously betray myself or pretend to be what I am not. I repeatedly ask myself in prayer, "Who am I, in truth?" God will answer by peeling off the layers of deception until it becomes obvious that this emperor has no clothes!

But we so often believe that the world (ourselves included) forces us to play our designated roles. In response to this misbelief, hear these words of encouragement:

Have the courage to be naked. You can only experience deep joy if you recognize and accept who you are and what has been planted in you. This is the call to live the life you have been given!

Descending to the depth of the heart can be liberating when we recognize and experience the whole of our desires, our wounds, our wrath, and our questions. Whatever you find there, always remember that God is gazing at you with love.

This way of speaking may sound unusual and abstract, but try to approach your creator deliberately and consciously. Imagine that he exists even if you have not been able to see or experience him. Take a look at what remains when your coat and shirt have been removed.

I admit this is challenging, and it may not work the first time. After all, we are talking about unadulterated truth, which presumes that we face the large and small lies of our life as well as our hiding places. In my own experience I sometimes feel cast out. I am cold until I realize that I am also exposed to the warmth of God's love—especially in my nakedness. God's welcome envelops me.

Without exposing ourselves in this unguarded manner, it is difficult to experience God's presence. A striking psychological theory comes to mind here: "We perceive everything according to our ability to perceive it." If we've failed to experience God, nothing will change unless we're willing to open ourselves to new experiences and realizations. Only when we experience the benevolent gaze of God toward us can we be transformed. Only then will we be able to let go of ourselves and perceive each other more truly and authentically.

We often regard ourselves and others differently than we truly are. I am frequently confronted with the images others have of me. They choose to believe what they wish to see: "Just wait. You'll make it big!" This thought is foreign to me, but many people think in such categories and willingly, or unwittingly, force them upon me. Though I've written many books, only a few people truly understand and accept me—not for what I've *done* but because of who I *am*. I am certainly not the only one who has had this experience.

These situations are not particularly disturbing as long as I know God's love in my life, which is linked to my own capacity to love myself and others.

The apostle John writes, "Everyone who loves is born of God and knows God" (1 Jn. 4:7). Only those who love selflessly in the same way that God does—God who became human in the person of Jesus—can begin to understand God's love.

Many people say: "I don't feel this love. I hear the words, dear Abbot Primate, but where is it in my life, this love of God?"

Truth and Love

Asking this question is a step toward love. Many people don't reach this point because they are too driven and preoccupied with inflating their egos. They are no longer in touch with their own existence in time.

We can't comprehend this love through logic or argument, just as we can't explain the color yellow to a blind person. We would literally have to give him sight. In much the same way, we must behold our lives with new eyes in order to hone our perception of God's love.

We are only capable of understanding love on an experiential level. If we take the time to sit with a homeless person and ask him how he came to be so, we may begin to care for someone whom others despise.

During a recent worship service, I found myself reacting negatively toward the person in front of me. I asked myself, "Why don't I like this person?" and reminded myself that he is loved by God just as I am; I had no reason to look down on him in any way. The remembrance of God's love brought me closer to this person, reinforcing the belief that the way toward truth in *my* life is bound up with the love and affection with which I encounter *others*.

Why should we bother with faith? Because faith makes a loving gaze toward myself and others possible.

The Truth and the Way

How are truth and what Jesus calls "the way" connected? God invites us to discover the truth through our journey with him.

Trust is essential. It isn't sufficient to say, "I only believe what I see; and only when I see will I proceed." A better way might be to say, "I only see what I believe." In faith as in life, the way emerges as we walk forward. We learn to recognize the truth as we journey with God.

Because the things that used to offer us a sense of security fall away when we set out on a journey, we must learn to engage our need for safety differently. When people ask me what my life will be like in five or ten years, I tell them I don't want to know; I don't need to plan so far ahead. In the New Testament, Jesus reminds us: "Do not worry about tomorrow, for tomorrow will bring worries of its own" (Matt. 6:34).

One of the many blessings of faith is its potential to pull us out of our need for certainty. We buy insurance for everything, even planning ahead to cover burial costs in order to make it safely underground!

In the final analysis, money drives our financial and material demand for security. We would do well to ask whether we really need so much. One of my uncles grabbed me around the throat after my high school graduation and said: "Why do you want to enter the monastery? You could make so much money. Money, real money!"

Puzzled, I looked at him and startled him with my response: "So what?"

Turning away from this need for security requires knowing very clearly what we want, which is a capacity we can't develop overnight. While it is possible to teach someone the multiplication table or a new language, learning to relinquish control involves a multitude of decisions each person makes alone. So I say again: "Let go and focus on small things. This way is possible and liberating!"

Faith plays an integral role. At some point the heart must make a connection with God. Nothing we do can make this happen. As unfair as it may sound, faith is a gift. Faith comes by grace; we can't bring it about on our own.

We also need the humility to receive. We deceive ourselves by thinking we don't need faith. Our connection to God cannot be earned, and attaining the humility necessary for faith can be a long, slow journey.

Some people come to faith as a result of a heart attack or illness. Such a crisis allows them to understand that nothing is certain. Visiting people in the hospital, I've often heard them ask, "What good is supposed to come of this?" It's an authentic question that can lead to deeper wisdom—particularly when we humble ourselves in the face of a life-altering experience.

Parents have a particular responsibility in the formation of the heart and can help their children develop an attitude of humility early on. Some children grow up with a sense of entitlement and an insatiable demand for instant gratification. Our children can also become a means for our own gratification as we shuffle them to ballet class, musical lessons, and various sports practices. Participation in these activities is not wrong, but we often fail to remember that children need time to develop in their own way and time. Our expectations often reflect the climate of achievement we ourselves cultivate.

Sometimes life needs room to unfold; children need time to make important discoveries and space to deepen their experiences.

Childhood can be a time when faith grows roots. Like other forms of learning, the discovery of faith requires time and attention and can enable the child to grow into an adult who doesn't need to be the center of the universe.

On the whole, I see a new attitude forging a path in our culture. I wrote earlier about the pressures of the business world, but many in that sphere have become more modest about their ambitions as they begin to recognize the suffering caused by the exploitation of people and the environment.

I have also seen this attitude emerge in some of my acquaintances, friends, and classmates as they scale back the demands on themselves and others. I was touched by how Frank-Walter Steinmeier, a leader in the Social Democratic Party in Germany, honored his wife's need by donating a kidney. Such a deed doesn't require a Christian mindset, but it demonstrates what it means to live with integrity, a vital dimension of faith. Did Mr. Steinmeier lose a kidney or did he gain a profound sense of connection to his wife? In a wonderful witness of generosity, he gave a part of himself so that she could live. Consider the example of Franz Müntefering, former chairman of the same political party and a leading industrialist, who took a leave from his responsibilities to care for his wife when she was dying of cancer. Such actions are remarkable and in accord with the values of the Christian faith.

A wonderful intimacy develops when we open completely to one another and are willing to give to and receive from each another. When we have the courage to stand before God just as we are, God helps us trace our way into the deepest truth of our lives. The journey starts with the first step we take toward God.

Living Meaning-fully

Life is endangered wherever people don't devote themselves to each other. It will not blossom in such an environment. Many people bide their time in precisely this kind of stultifying atmosphere as a result of stress at work, the pressure of both parents working away from home, or the conflicts that arise between couples about money or the lack of attention. Each of us has the power to create life-altering change in situations like these.

We must first learn to listen to our life and recognize that what the world offers often creates unrest within us and between us. When we step back, we can discover what inner freedom and a different approach to life can offer. We can find a way to transform what has been given to us, however incomplete it may seem, and discover something whole and meaningful.

I experienced this with a couple who were expecting a child diagnosed with Down's Syndrome. Many people encouraged them to get an abortion, but they consciously chose to have the child. While it was a taxing decision, their family experiences great joy because of the gift of this special child.

Having a disabled child can be difficult because of society's lack of acceptance, and telling parents not to let it bother them can be an added burden. Those who vehemently argue against abortion without knowing how difficult it can be to raise a disabled child sidestep the reality the parents will face. This is the point at which faith as a personal journey with God becomes real. As we trust God more deeply, we discover that not only will we manage this unique task, but we will also grow through it, be blessed by it, and derive meaning from it in our lives.

When we accept that Jesus is "the life," our standards and values begin to shift. Still, we might wonder what good will come of having a disabled child and taking on a responsibility that will make life more difficult. We might even think, "What right does a monk have to talk to me about the depth of being?"

Yes, this is a difficult circumstance, but the path of least resistance seldom leads anywhere worth going. True joy doesn't spring from choices made out of convenience.

We usually imagine a vacation as a time when we are free to do nothing. While this may be the case for two or three days, we soon become restless. Human beings aren't made for leisure alone, and as much as we like to think doing nothing will eliminate the stress in our lives, that is seldom the case. Making a concrete plan and being able to check things off a list can be satisfying, much like developing a plan for the way we will live our life.

What matters is not convenience but meaning—the joy that evolves from a calling, the joy that a disabled child can bring despite the strain, and the greater depth that emerges because of the journey itself.

Yes, I am taking aim at our entertainment-driven culture. Is Christian faith still relevant in our time? A purely intellectual approach to faith can't provide a sufficient answer, and faith isn't particularly fashionable—a fact made plain by people's indifference toward God. Why is this so?

Over time, faith has been reduced to a few controversial questions such as contraception, abortion, divorce, celibacy, and the ordination of women. Many among us reject the church's stance toward such questions, but these perennial themes continue to surface in debates about faith in Western culture, as if Christianity consisted of nothing more. Of course these questions are important and play a role in our lives, but it's simplistic to push aside personal faith because the church's response to these issues is perceived as antiquated. Topical discussions remain inadequate in addressing the meaning of God for each human life. Debating difficult and intriguing questions of faith doesn't necessarily move us to the heart of the matter.

If I've veered off the road in my car, I don't care about the scratches and dents but about whether the engine still runs so that I can drive. So, too, the engine that drives every human life is our personal connection with God; it must be functional. As is the case with human relationships, there will always be scratches and dents along the way. In terms of our relationship with God, these dents might take the form of things I can't or don't want to understand.

The Question of Meaning

Many people in our society are happy without faith. They believe they have all they need and lead a good life; I don't mean to discredit that. Faith just isn't relevant for them. In days gone by, one could preach a juicy hellfire and brimstone sermon to wake such people from their indifference; they'd feel guilty about their lives and perhaps go to confession. But this tactic seldom works anymore, and I wonder whether such an approach was ever truly effective.

The notion that people turn away from faith when things are going well is, to a certain extent, true. This saddens me because God also grants the good things we have in life.

Those who dwell on the sunny side of life may enjoy it heartily, but the question of meaning is still real. Like all of us, they need to question their aim in life, the destination of their journey, and the meaning that comes from their way of life.

While my aim is not to recount only sad stories, listening to them can be telling. When I'm faced with a circumstance I can't handle, the fragility of my constructs becomes obvious unless I'm anchored to something greater than myself. For example, what does the future mean for a couple whose child dies or commits suicide? Do they have a foundation that can support them? Are their lives grounded in a reality that includes but also transcends them?

Superficial joy is fine and good, but it becomes fragile when we find ourselves dealing with questions of deeper meaning or facing experiences that bring us to the edge of what we know. In such circumstances, the wisdom of faith can be enormously helpful to those who know of a truth that transcends ordinary life.

What is the meaning of life? If we are going to face this question, Jesus's calling to make meaning of suffering and death—what the apostle Paul called the "sting" of our humanity—is fundamental. Jesus embodies meaning by standing for truth in and through his own death, not only defeating death but also healing those who are ill in body and soul.

Every time we feel that God is reaching out to us, we are in the presence of grace. I remember the story of an accomplished man who lived abroad for many years. During that time he met people who shared their faith with him, and he began to read the Bible with great interest. Though he couldn't explain the shift his life had begun to take, he felt touched in a profound way. If it was possible that the Bible was true, he had to go deeper. He knew the context of his life would change completely because his existence would no longer be confined to a given number of years on earth. He had come to set his life in the broader framework of eternity. Most of us sense that something transcends the finitude of our existence.

Do you believe in eternity? If not, try to consider it a possibility and see what happens in both your mind and your heart. You might find yourself questioning your assumption that eternity doesn't exist or interest you, given the constructive implications eternity might hold for your life now.

As people who spend weeks paging through travel brochures or deliberating over the purchase of a new car, we should matter enough to ourselves to consider the question of eternity when we contemplate the meaning of life.

Real and lasting joy can't be had without cost, and I don't mind repeating myself when I say that what brings true happiness is living the life God intends for us, which is contrary to the beliefs our culture promotes. We must fundamentally rethink our attitude toward life.

A little soul massage here or a beautiful worship service there is hardly enough! We must learn to love others even when it is difficult and painful. Love is a demanding but revolutionary act, especially in a world full of need.

Regardless of faith, all sorts of people generously donate money and time to humanitarian causes. The Christian faith, however, uniquely incorporates the need for meaning that so many people yearn for, whether consciously or not. This alone is reason enough to believe! As Christians we bind ourselves to others and discover a *way* that points toward something greater than ourselves.

This dimension of meaning is not part of a merit system that secures our ticket to heaven. Meaning develops as a result of opening up toward God and other people. But if this is so important, why is it so difficult?

I have come to believe that many people feel patronized by the church. They don't want church authorities telling them what to do; they don't want someone dictating what happens in the privacy of their bedroom. People want the freedom to act independently without being restricted by the church. In some regards, I can empathize. We need to have more confidence in believers, keeping this insight in mind:

No one has to believe in God in order to be decent and good, but if I believe in God, I am invited—and finally compelled—to live in this way.

Those touched by God can no longer go about their day-to-day life as if the way they live doesn't matter. Inevitably, they will need to ask important questions that explore matters related both to their daily lives and also their responsibility toward the world. Faith is diminished when it is exiled to the arena of private piety.

The church's tradition of devotion to Mary illustrates how faith changes the way we live. People more concerned with ambition may find this sort of devotion unnecessary, but is a lucrative career and prestige enough? These things may bring success, but will they offer authentic and lasting happiness?

We might try to tell ourselves that such aspirations are enough; this is all we want in life. God does not impose himself on anyone, and we must not try to make people feel guilty in order to get them to believe. However, we should try to open their eyes to the evil that selfish actions, such as the recent global financial crisis, can cause.

Look again at the text from the apostle Paul's First Letter to Timothy. What if we shared these verses with the people who work in the context of this crisis? It might challenge them to see the financial crisis as a crisis of values and pressing ethical questions. They might even see that fundamental values in human relationships were dramatically and tragically disregarded.

If faith continues to disappear, its absence will continue to affect our society and economy. Other factors besides the illusion of invincibility and a calculated devotion to profit must direct our behavior. In the wake of such false paths, we must find our way to the sustaining system of values that Christianity offers.

We also need the witness of people who have found meaning in their lives through accountability to God. Such a *way* is grounded in love for others; it is demonstrated in both large and small ways, regardless of our comfort.

Recognizing Beauty

Faith is not like a suit we put on for church each Sunday. It settles into our marrow. Unfortunately, we lack compelling voices within the church able to communicate this truth.

I want to break free of the stereotypes regarding the church and Christianity because I know that living by faith can effect much good for individuals and for society. I want to shout this message from the rooftops, gladly standing with others in order to bear witness to the beauty of this way.

In order to accomplish this, we need to consider different forms of communication in a wide range of disciplines and arenas. A recent discussion in the book-publishing world centered on authors with the ability to turn a typical reading into a genuine performance. When I watch André Rieu in concert on television and the camera scans the audience, I can see how he delights people with his music by the way he engages the audience. Or consider the way a sporting event evokes strong participation and powerful emotions: fans shed tears of joy and grief in the face of triumph and defeat.

My great desire is to demonstrate this faith in new, gripping, and relevant ways. We need to seriously consider how we can draw on the great beauty that this faith entails.

The issue of communication isn't a matter of either/or but rather both/and. Certainly we must continue to rely on traditional approaches, but we must also utilize new forms in order to reach more people, particularly the younger generation. The fact that our churches are poorly attended reveals the number of people who no longer see faith as relevant for their lives.

I am personally compelled by the need to convey the beauty of truth through music. Music can touch the hidden recesses of the soul in a way that speech does not. I understand Pope Emeritus Benedict's passion for Mozart's masses; I myself derive great joy from Gregorian chant. As human beings, we celebrate life with all our senses. In the intricate patterns of Bach or lively newer genres, we can learn to engage our whole heart through rhythm and melody. In the process, we might debunk the preconceived notion that faith is ultimately boring.

Imagine the difference between such a performance and the way the church is routinely perceived.

What matters is God. We begin to hear his voice when, as Pope Emeritus Benedict described it, we turn down the frequencies of other channels. God transmits quietly on his own channel within us.

Believing with Head and Heart

How do we believe? Faith in God cannot be forced, not even through the most ingenious use of reason. Authentic faith must be discovered so that we can perceive its beauty.

Of course reason is necessary, lest we fall prey to simple-mindedness or, worse, heresy. But while reason is a great and necessary gift from God, we will never grasp the mystery of faith through reason alone. Though the capacity for faith remains in our society today—including all manner of remedies, crystals, and cures—rare indeed is faith in God.

Faith is intrinsically bound up with our human relationships. The other cannot be fully known if I am unwilling to give myself fully. The full measure of great love cannot be experienced apart from vulnerability. I come to recognize the character of the other by reflecting on their life. Reason can help us recognize when love is no longer mutual or when we're being used. In this way, the issue of faith is necessarily relational, decided in part by how we participate in all of our relationships.

Don't settle for too little. Seek to discover the beauty, fullness, freedom, and perspective that our faith offers. God doesn't desire to restrict or impoverish our life, though we may have felt or feared this in the past.

Our image of faith is tied to biography and experience. Though increasingly rare, faith is transmitted through the mediation of family, friends, and clergy.

Allow me to illustrate my point: suppose you hated math because you couldn't stand your teacher. If your instructor did a poor job of explaining the subject, you would need to recognize the value of math in some other way, especially if you hoped to become an engineer. Many parents wrestle with finding a way to communicate with their children about matters of faith, but what ultimately matters is their own personal encounter with God. That being said, we don't believe alone; we believe together. Other Christians brings encouragement and joy. Faith lives in community, not in the proverbial ivory tower.

Unfortunately, much has gone awry in the church's history. I feel the burden of the many errors that have been made in the transmission of our faith through the centuries. I sometimes wonder whether authorities in the church are really bothered by the injustices that have been perpetrated in the name of God, if they consider the many human lives that have been destroyed. An extreme example is the burning of witches—or think of the Inquisition! Thank God these are matters of the past, and hopefully we've learned from our mistakes. But the wounds still ache, and these atrocities deter many people from believing today.

If we are honest, we will recognize that missteps are inevitable because the church is made up of human beings; the wounds remain.

This realization requires great humility, which is a challenge for many. But I believe we witnessed a positive development in the example of Pope Emeritus Benedict, who intentionally practices humility. He still envisions the Catholic Church as a system of small cells, much like it was in the early church. Hopefully this vision will help cast the image of the church and the Christian faith in a renewed and constructive light.

Returning to Modesty

We should neither overwhelm the church nor ourselves in this endeavor. Christ did not say we would gather the masses around us but that we ought to be leaven in the world, the salt of the earth, and a light in the darkness. While the way of humility is our path, our posture should not be one of retreat. Being humble doesn't mean hiding our light under a bushel basket; it means being present to others without making demands. It means relating a clear and loving message without triumphalism, arrogance, or domination.

Our call to humility, as well as our approach to sharing our faith, involves each individual and the broader traditions of the church. The inherent worth of our message offers a strong foundation for life.

All of us face temptations. Within the context of our consumer culture, the lure of material possessions perpetually beguiles us. Whether we covet our neighbor's house or hunger for more possessions and money, our insatiable desires and the pressures of our work can occupy all of our energy, leaving little or no room for God. In the face of countless temptations, such longings are continuously stimulated. What would I do if I found several million dollars lying on the ground with no one around to see me take it? Aren't we often drawn to an attractive man or a beautiful woman? What does it take to resist this attraction, to find the strength to stay with our chosen partner?

It is far better to register our full humanity than to repress the desire stirred up in such circumstances. We need to learn to perceive without judgment; pushing temptations beyond our immediate reach won't solve the problem or add beauty to our lives. Living in a perpetual state of repression will eventually backfire, resulting in injury to ourselves and others.

I know a family that lives according to Christ's words in the Lord's Prayer, "Give us this day our daily bread." They don't accumulate riches but do spend a great deal of time with their children to ensure that they thrive. Though the same temptations confront them, this family chooses a way of life that brings them great happiness and satisfaction.

If we dare to attempt this journey, we may be surprised to discover how much affirmation and satisfaction can be found from people who secretly share our desire. Faith becomes concrete as we consciously and persistently choose this path in the face of temptations to do otherwise.

The fact that faith involves difficult decisions demonstrates that a life of freedom is both beautiful and hard. Let's return to the example of desiring another person while in a committed relationship. It can be tempting to imagine life with a different partner, even while happily married. Yet if we have experienced the way a spouse can carry us in a critical moment of need, we will find the strength to remain steadfast. Clear water is only found in a well dug deep. Once we taste this water from the source, we can more easily resist the murky temptations that precede it. Life offers us many good and beautiful things, but Jesus speaks of one treasure worth more than we could ever accumulate or achieve: "The kingdom of heaven is like treasure hidden in a field, which someone found and hid; then in his joy he goes and sells all he has and buys that field" (Matt. 13:44).

It is important to care for and tend this treasure. One way is to offer a loving gaze. When we see each other early in the morning do we focus on messy hair and wrinkles, or do we gaze lovingly at the inner beauty that fascinates and supports us?

I am reminded of the expression "staying in touch," which beautifully captures the need to maintain contact that is both external and internal. In the same way that we choose to sustain a connection with others, we also must decide time and again to live a life of faith in and with God. Only then can we experience faith in all its beauty.

Brimming with Joy

Do you associate Christian faith with fullness of life? Christ spells out this fullness when he says, "I came that they may have life, and have it abundantly" (John 10:10).

Unfortunately, the church doesn't always fulfill its potential or invite others to experience this abundance. Some hear such a promise and imagine life in a religious order, especially a strict order that they presume equates Christian life with renunciation of joy as well as suffering and pain. But this presumption is not the case in monastic communities. St. Benedict voices the invitation of Christ with beautiful simplicity: "What is more delightful than [the] Lord calling to us? See how the Lord in his love shows us the way of life" (RB Prol. 19–20). The call to monastic life is an invitation to receive a measure of this fullness.

Living in fullness means living in the presence of God, but first we must become conscious of God's presence. The admonitions we should follow are relatively simple: love God and others; live with integrity; act honestly toward all; do what is good; and act with justice. These are the foundational principles for human living and are not overly difficult to put into practice.

In the prologue to his Rule, St. Benedict cites Psalm 34 when he speaks to those entering monastic life: "Which of you desires life, and covets many days to enjoy good? Keep your tongue from evil, and your lips from speaking deceit. Depart from evil, and do good; seek peace, and pursue it!" (Prol. 12–14).

In order to be able to enjoy life fully, we need to make a shift from the material to what I call the relational plane. This radical break moves us away from the relentless striving for possessions that seems to characterize modern life—away from the yearning for a larger flat screen television, a newer car model, and ever more exotic vacations. While I don't begrudge people what they have, life is about more than the fulfillment of material desires. People with many possessions can have many worries. If I were to wish harm on someone, it might be that they acquire large sums of money. The pressure to invest it effectively and the worry about losing it all can become an incessant preoccupation.

We often hear that people who win the lottery don't end up being happy. Studies suggest that the joy of such fortune tends to last several months before the winner returns to the level of happiness they experienced before they won the jackpot. Often they find themselves even less happy than they were before. While these first months might be enjoyable, will they lead to true happiness that lasts?

It's a paradox, isn't it? We know that money can't make us happy, and yet we continue to run after it.

If we are not oriented toward God, it can be extraordinarily difficult to let go of striving for material things. St. Benedict identifies orientation toward God as the path to a fulfilled life. The church has made, and continues to make, the mistake of giving people the impression that the path to a fuller life is cluttered with lists of obligations we *must* do and warnings about what we *must not* do. These lists often require us to suppress our wishes while constricting our desires.

Whole generations have grown up with this image of a forbidding God. I believe many younger people perceive faith as unattractive because they don't recognize its relevance in their experience. Unfortunately, what they have experienced has been neither inviting nor beneficial. Many people associate faith only with the notion that they are prevented from sleeping in on Sundays and are required to participate in strange rituals they don't fully understand.

The idea that a faithful person can't enjoy life is fundamentally flawed. Even some theologians fall into this trap. I once sat at a table with a Protestant theologian who launched an angry tirade against Roman Catholics by saying, "Look at how much Catholicism exaggerates joy, allowing so much heathenism into the faith that it amounts to a subversion of true Christianity." I responded by saying that his purely intellectual, sober-minded approach to our wonderful, enlivening, and life-affirming faith struck me as an attempt to transplant a joyous Christianity into the rainy, foggy clime of Germany.

Our faith does not oppose the senses and neither does it disapprove of desire. It simply adds a decisive component to all aspects of life—a proper responsibility.

In popular culture, for instance, the meaning of sexuality is often reduced and ultimately desecrated, sold on the cheap even though the creator affirms that it should be lived and enjoyed fully and responsibly. The same is true for delicious food and the many other sensual gifts God gives us. All of these gifts can be used and enjoyed, even esteemed. God invites us to savor the sunny side of life, even wealth itself, but these gifts serve as an invitation to the practice of genuine responsibility for others. Such enjoyments are meant to expand gratitude in our lives. Everything may be permissible, but not everything is useful, as the apostle Paul puts it (see 1 Cor. 6:12).

We also need to consider the opposite approach: can a path *without* God be truly fulfilling?

Luck in Misfortune

Many viewed the Love Parade, an electronic dance music festival, as the paradigm for life in its fullness until a terrible disaster occurred in Duisburg, Germany, killing twenty-one people by suffocation and injuring more than 500 more. I am entirely in favor of people having fun together, and young people in particular should have a chance to let loose. But where were people drawn when catastrophe struck? The church!

Where else can we turn for comfort? I'd much prefer young people to be in church all the time, not only when terrible tragedies strike. We should let all people know that God is there for us in good times but also when sadness permeates our life. God is with us come what may! I especially want young people to know that the inherent meaning and well-being in a life with God is always available, not just when terrible things happen and we are at our wit's end.

The example of Duisburg shows that life is about more than having fun, which is limited in its capacity to make us happy. Fun isn't necessarily equated with fullness of life and can end in a moment, with unforeseen consequences. Being fully alive and experiencing true joy encompasses more than momentary pleasures.

Experiencing life in a full, embodied way often takes place in the context of community. We come together not only in times of desperate need but also in order to celebrate.

Why do people go to church? Certainly not because they wish to be bored. I recently played a concert with my rock band. While making arrangements for the concert, a parish associate asked if I would celebrate mass beforehand. I agreed and was astonished to find the enormous sanctuary filled to capacity. The parish associate later wrote me to say that more people gathered for that concert than for Christmas Eve services! I believe this was due to the fact that our performance conveyed something people expect from worship—namely, a real joy and affirmation of life.

Please pay attention to that last sentence: Christian faith means affirming life and living joyfully. Being a Christian isn't only about renunciation and the keeping of commandments. While these acts are a beneficial part of the journey, a multitude of gifts make up a faith that brings happiness and joy. I want to tell you about these gifts.

Because many people primarily associate faith with renunciation, I want to focus on how faith affirms life. But where do we find such affirmations in daily life?

Suppose I'm facing a difficult situation; I pause to say a brief prayer and realize I feel better. I often have this experience when I pray at the start of a long workday or face a difficult conversation. Throughout the day I am often distracted and don't recognize until evening that the situations turned out better than I imagined they would. I am not suggesting I always experience this feeling, but God regularly affirms my day-to-day experience, thereby affirming my life.

The Art of Celebration

God puts a high value on celebration. Throughout the Old Testament, he practically commands his people to pause and celebrate what he has done for them. But this experience extends beyond ancient times; Jews and Christians today celebrate many religious festivals, and most of our national holidays are based on events in the Christian calendar.

The origins of many feasts can be found in the church's life. What we call Carnival, or Mardi Gras, is an ancient Christian celebration. Originally the focus was on eating one's fill and celebrating one more time before the beginning of Lent. The German word for this festival is *Fastnacht*, "night of fasting," because it took place on the night preceding Ash Wednesday.

Too often Christians and the church relinquish experiences that are integral to the faith. These experiences remind us how the church is oriented toward community. As Christians, we have ample reason to celebrate! Community is the heart of the church and needs to be celebrated.

We shouldn't limit ourselves merely to conducting worship; rather, we should find ways to celebrate God through joyful occasions that create community. For Christians, piety cannot be seen or experienced as a strictly private affair. The church's celebration of the Eucharist is essentially communal, even though some people might prefer to retreat to a quiet corner and attend mass as an observer. The language we use to describe this celebration—we "read mass"—reinforces the idea of faith being a personal, and not particularly exciting, event.

I have two beautiful memories concerning the power of celebration and fellowship at our monastery of St. Ottilien. In 1980, we celebrated the 1500th anniversary of St. Benedict's birth and wanted to somehow honor the occasion. I suggested we throw a big public party to thank the people who live nearby for all they had done to help us over the years. The celebration began with a special outdoor mass; afterward we treated everyone to homemade rolls, bread, cake, and other local specialties prepared in our own monastery kitchen. The monastery brass ensemble played, and some of the brothers played fun games with the children. The festival was so successful it became an annual event. In fact, we had to stop advertising because the crowds were more than we could handle. The regular rhythms of our monastery were put on hold so that all of the monks could be involved in the festivities. This new tradition reminds us that people enjoy festivals, particularly when they promote community and enjoyment. Celebration, indeed!

My second example involves a young monk who offered a Vespers prayer service for the young people in the community. The service quickly became a tradition, taking place on the first Friday of each month in the small baroque chapel at the monastery. I suggested that we hold the service in the large monastery church so that the entire monastic community could attend, but he objected, pointing out that "the chapel is so cozy" for this particular service.

"You and your cozy corners!" I replied, but let him proceed with his plans. As time passed, more and more young people attended the event. Sixteen years after its modest beginning, the monk in charge came to me and said: "Father Abbot, the monks will have to hold Compline (the monastic service of nightly prayer) in the Chapter House and not in the church; the young people have taken over the church—it's jam-packed."

"I have been waiting a long time for this day," I replied, laughing. Since then, up to a thousand young people have attended this special Vespers service at St. Ottilien without any advertisement on our part. Celebration, indeed!

Why do they come? What are they looking for? The experience of community goes hand in hand with prayer, spiritual experience, and a shared sense of the presence of God. This kind of celebration mirrors the deep enjoyment of life that is at the heart of our faith. No wonder the experience has a lasting impact on young people and a deeper reach than a party soaked with beer.

I visited the Taizé Community in Burgundy, France, the year before their beloved founder, Father Roger, died. During that time I witnessed the throngs of young people standing in line after the evening service and kneeling in order to receive his blessing. I also approached him and introduced myself. He was delighted to meet me, and we later spent time talking about the resurrection. Brother Roger lived his faith with deep engagement and joy. The special outreach to youth in this community was his vision, and Taizé continues to be a place that touches many thousands of young people each year. They gather with great anticipation and joy, sensing the integrity of this community's faith. Celebration indeed!

These examples suggest that joyful forms of religious life can be part of our experience and that true spiritual hunger for God exists. Just because we haven't experienced such things doesn't mean they aren't real.

But patience is required. Living life in its fullness suggests giving people and events room and time to grow in their own way. It might mean allowing yourself to be inspired by the witness of a man like Brother Roger—a joy rooted in fellowship with God and other Christians—and shaped by his vision of resurrection. It sometimes helps to tell yourself, "Sit down and imagine that you will die and then rise again!" This truth far exceeds the victory of a favorite soccer team, though for many people it may be an abstract concept to grasp.

Joy the Whole World Over

In Germany, one often senses that the very utterance of the word "God" evokes a guilty conscience. We have largely lost what was once a natural way of relating to God and expressing our faith, in part because we continue to be burdened by the legacy of the Enlightenment.

As Abbot Primate of the Benedictines I get to travel the world. The approach to faith and life I see in other countries is often refreshing and delightful. I believe we can we learn something from these communities. We might find in their witness a more natural way of interacting with God in daily life. For many of these people, the reality of God is an integral part of their experience. This integrated relationship with the divine can be seen in other religions as well. A discussion about Indian philosophy or theology can be misleading because one can only speak about the faith of people in a holistic sense. Faith cannot be separated from daily life or distinguished from the way people think and act—a dichotomy that exists primarily in Western culture.

The history of this separation began centuries before Christ. The pre-Socratic philosophers questioned the traditional Greek belief system prevalent in their day; they wanted to discover if the assertion that human beings were the center of the world was true. They wanted to find wisdom through their own ability to reason, which is still the case today. Reason is regarded as the determining criterion to which faith must be subjected. Historically during this time, Greece experienced a break between the common faith of the populace and the schools of philosophical belief. As a result, Socrates was accused of atheism.

Nevertheless, people from countries such as Spain are often less inhibited in their faith, though even this cannot be taken for granted. The United States also seems to possess a greater spontaneity than Europe in terms of how people live their faith. Perhaps the legacy of the first settlers, who experienced many hardships and endured with the help of their faith, contributes to this lack of inhibition. This is not unlike what Germany experienced in the wake of World War II. Prayers for food were habitual given the widespread hunger people experienced. Today we simply buy what we need; we no longer think we need God to survive. This shift also explains the image of God as a divine being relegated to the margins rather than a necessary reality we call upon in everyday life.

When we grapple with our faith it helps to realize that we inhabit a small place in the world. We should also guard against the arrogance of regarding our life and faith as the absolute measure of experience. Encountering joy in the lives of others might astonish us. Life in its fullness! Our Western approach to life and sense of identity certainly don't represent a cure for the world. What can the so-called "developing world" teach us about regaining a measure of this joy and vitality of faith?

Reason and Feeling

Vitality reveals itself when we consider the fragility of our current way of life. We need reason in order to function as a society, and it is imperative for the advance of science. We also acknowledge that scientific explanations dealing with origins of the world and human evolution are not matters of faith, even though these approaches are interesting and important. As human beings, however, we are not simply biological creatures; we are creative beings with values, dreams, and desires who perpetually search for meaning within and beyond the confines of this life. We often lack a sense of joy within the scope of human experience because we consider this feeling unscientific.

Some neurophysiologists suggest that feelings and desires are merely triggered by chemical processes in our brain. While this may be true, what is the undergirding foundation of these processes? At the root of our feelings of love we certainly reckon with bodily experiences. We might even say that these experiences make love possible in the first place. I find the neurophysiological approach on its own offers little comfort. Can we accept the premise that nothing lies behind our experience of human life except a set of indifferent physiological processes? Why do religious feelings exist? Doesn't the reality of our spiritual experience extend beyond the empirical world?

According to the theory of evolution, we evolve as creatures in ways that are shaped by our need for survival. Yet religious feelings appear to be part of a collective experience across cultures, not merely a placebo for our fears. An added dimension resides within us. While those working in the natural sciences make helpful and relevant discoveries, we must acknowledge that science is not sufficient in itself to make sense of human life. Allowing such an approach to define our experience increases the risk of one-dimensional thinking. As a result we blind ourselves to the other realities that shape our lives.

Please don't misunderstand: reason matters, but we often give it too much weight. By focusing on an empirical perspective we fail to sense the richness of other dimensions of reality.

Reason is part of faith; it is a gift from God. But we cannot fit faith into the structure of reason. Faith and reason exist in tension with each other, forming a frame of reference we did not create. Having been brought into being by God with both reason and faith, we can believe in an entirely irrational manner or live as if reason alone matters.

Balance, ultimately, is what is important. If we ignore reason altogether, we face the danger of falling prey to superstition and are vulnerable to the kind of cruelties that took place in the Middle Ages. In our culture, reason has come to play a regulatory function, helping us recognize and curb unreasonable and zealous acts that run counter to true faith.

We also recognize that people facing difficult struggles are more likely to pray than others. Faith offers comfort and genuine security. Trials evoke fear and can lead to unhealthy ways of dealing with the challenges we face. In such cases, a refusal to use reason can be dangerous, leading us in unhelpful or even destructive directions. In the face of trials, people sometimes consult ghosts and ancestors, looking beyond God for help or clarity. The fear that drives these choices is sometimes to blame.

Believers influenced by this sort of irrationality sometimes blame illness on another human being—as we find in the case of bewitching or the evil eye. Superstitions like these are still prevalent just beneath the surface, even in modern societies like ours. Those people susceptible to superstition are sometimes less encumbered and more open toward another spiritual dimension of life, but in being so they turn a blind eye to rationality. In contrast, those accustomed to the tendencies of modernity often limit themselves to the dimension of reason. Both practices are imbalanced and unhelpful when it comes to grasping the expanse of our lives in the presence of God as understood by faith.

Joy in faith begins when I choose to cease living by reason alone and open myself to the wider dimensions of faith.

Finding Inner Peace

People who turn to God during hard times often recount how God gifted them with a sense of protection. The security that comes from God manifests itself in a deep peace and equanimity amid the many fears of daily life. Certainly, there's an abundance of fear to go around: the fear of losing a job or being unable to maintain a certain social status, not having enough money to live well, losing a marriage partner, facing a serious and unexpected illness, or seeing a loved one suffer.

God promises to give us the deepest sense of belonging, together with true equanimity and inner peace in the circumstances of our utterly ordinary human life. Good news, indeed!

My rock band plays a song called "My Best Friend," which deals precisely with this issue: we need friends in this world. Yet when things fall apart we sometimes have the bitter experience of watching people turn away until only a faithful few remain. Things may even get so bad that everyone abandons us. Nevertheless, One abides who will grant us a sense of safety, One who will not abandon us when all the rest turn away. In Matthew, Jesus says: "Remember, I am with you always, to the end of the age" (Matt. 28:20). The prophet Isaiah puts it this way: "Can a woman forget her nursing child, or show no compassion for the child of her womb?" (Isa. 49:15).

These texts are extremely relevant. How many of us feel abandoned or forsaken by a mother, father, spouse, or trusted friend? Though we highly value our independence and individuality, we often become quite lonely as a result. Loneliness can be a real problem in our fast-paced and individualistic society. We no longer live in multi-generational households. The number of single households continues to increase, and loneliness is far too prevalent, especially among the older generation.

In our time, children often leave their hometowns and move to cities. Many who live in high-rise apartment buildings don't know their neighbors. Even in such conditions, the light of God's love can enter our hearts when we consciously embrace the reality that someone is holding us like a trusted friend.

It's not uncommon for people to think: "I'm not that old; loneliness doesn't relate to me." True, when we're young or in midlife we find ourselves dealing with different problems like the pressures of work or a chronic shortage of time. How, then, can faith offer us equanimity and inner peace when we find ourselves driven by day-to-day stresses? How can faith help families in which both parents are working?

Faith can't and doesn't need to offer immediate security in every moment, but it can provide something like a roof over the house of our lives. We might not even notice it's there. It's like a child at home playing. The mother is there, but the child doesn't need to see her to feel safe; she feels her mother's presence and can play in peace. However, when the mother briefly leaves the house, the child immediately notices and feels less secure. I offer this image as a way to suggest that the gift of protection is part and parcel of faith, an assurance that is always at work.

It is the same when we pray: we don't need to prepare our hearts with a great effort. Think of it as turning to talk with God who has been there all along.

How do we communicate the image of the protective roof or the child in the calming presence of her mother to people who are perpetually driven? I sometimes want to say, "Stop running around and sit down under the shade of a tree!"

Get Off the Hamster Wheel

Living habitually in the passing lane is one of the biggest problems of our time. Many people in our communities feel anxious because too much is expected of them or they've taken on too much.

Is this surprising? I am concerned about our tendency to drive ourselves into the ground. Contemporary job conditions can also induce stress, making it even more difficult to escape. Being required to multi-task and not being able to focus on one task is profoundly stressful, but we must recognize how we collude in creating these conditions and do what we can to change them. We have more power to change these situations than we often think we do.

I derive great solace from knowing there is someone behind the scenes who walks with me. He is simply there, even when I don't take notice. In light of this presence, stress is no longer a meaningless challenge. In fact, I sometimes suspect this sense of meaninglessness is the worst thing about stress.

We create a terrific amount of stress for ourselves, like a caged hamster running on the wheel. If the wheel doesn't spin the hamster is out of sorts. We get used to this drive over time, both psychologically and biologically, and are unable to face it until we quiet down. What can we do to remedy this imbalance? In his Rule, St. Benedict gives monks a set order for the day so that no matter what work we do we can anchor ourselves in prayer and slow our spinning.

Monastic rules can be applied to every person's life. We might decide to begin each day in prayer, allow the day to be interrupted at set times by prayer, and end the day in prayer. This rhythm makes us more mindful of God and can create a sense of harmony for the pounding bass line that shapes the day's work.

This agenda requires making a conscious decision against being pushed about by a stressful daily schedule. Someone recently told me about a group hiking in the mountains. They scrambled up the mountains and were proud of their accomplishment. When they returned someone asked if they had seen the beautiful flowers in the mountain meadows. No, they hadn't. All they had focused on was their effort to reach the top. People create stress for themselves even in their leisure, allowing the world to pass by unnoticed.

We can't entirely escape the pressures of our achievement-oriented society. It surrounds us, and we must face it. But we must take a more active role in shaping our society and the lives we lead—consciously and unconsciously. We should take note of the things we do have the influence to change. We might try to step on the brakes from time to time or neglect the habit of chasing every task. We might even get off the bicycle and take in the beauty of the landscape!

How can we develop intentional habits of slowing down? First, we must want to do so. Maybe we need to experience how good it feels when someone else says, "That's enough for now; I'm going to take time to reflect." A group of managers have started taking weekend retreats in monasteries, giving themselves time for silence and space for longer, structured exercises. Some are nervous at the start because nothing seems to be happening. This lack of results fuels the drive they experience in their daily lives: they are unable to abide without having something to do.

Others extract themselves from their daily grind to attend monastic retreats and recognize within themselves a growing desire to stay. They perceive how solitude and prayer invite them to come home to themselves and to God in ways that are not possible amid the constant drive of their day-to-day life. Although firmly planted in the world with the responsibilities of families and jobs, they discover and become much more themselves in the quiet. When this happens, some even consider quitting their job the next morning.

While each of us bears responsibility for ourselves and others, our longing for solitude is real, as it has been for many who came before us. Great spiritual leaders—such as St. Gregory the Great (d. 604), St. Bernard of Clairvaux (d. 1153), and St. Hugh of Cluny (d. 1109)—also had to contend with the need for solitude and a call to be present for others.

Each of these men desired a deeply contemplative life but ended up "dancing at every wedding at once," as we say in German. That is, their work as spiritual leaders entailed its own kind of stress, the result of which was a perpetual longing for deeper solitude. But I'm convinced that their drive was also their strength, allowing them to found monasteries and lead the church in difficult times. St. Hugh of Cluny was present at the great encounter of Pope Gregory VII and King Henry IV at Canossa, influencing the Pope to show greater mercy to Henry and free him from his ban. During St. Hugh's lifetime, the dukes broke their allegiances with the king because of this ban and exploited the situation by refusing to cooperate with an excommunicated king, thereby expanding their local hold on power.

In his old age, St. Hugh retired to a small monastery not far from Cluny, where he had overseen the building of the third abbey church. After he entered the monastery he seldom left it, apparently because he no longer had the strength to deal with the stress.

Learning to Let Go

What does this mean for us today? I am suggesting that our problem with stress is hardly a new phenomenon and that walking away from our responsibilities is not an appropriate solution. The discovery of slowness as a way of life isn't of itself sufficient.

Certainly the idea of solitude is alluring, especially given the ambitious nature of our lives in modern society. If we lack solitude we experience a great longing for it. But consider the possibility of attaining a sense of peace and quiet without experiencing happiness. What then?

If you notice feeling less at home with yourself—if you have less time and patience for others and for God—it's time to learn the art of letting go. Take a break from some activities and give yourself time away from others. Find the space to laugh.

I need space to find a sense of quiet in my own life, and that requires not taking myself too seriously!

You might counter this idea by saying, "I have to make sure that my co-workers are doing their job, and I have so many things to do around the house." No, you don't. Some people live under the assumption that not only do they need to have every problem under control, but they must also solve everyone else's problems as well. If we allow others to be responsible and work their problems out on their own, we may discover they are far better suited to this task than we are. We don't have to do it all, for ourselves or for others. Our insistence to do so simply reveals that we only trust ourselves. As we learn to trust God, we find ourselves learning to trust others.

The Freeing Power of Forgiveness

The art of letting go encompasses the ability to let go of our trespasses as well as those of others. In fact, we must let them go because clinging to them binds and robs us of inner freedom.

It is always a tragedy when one person hurts another through slander or abusive behavior. Many church leaders have yet to recognize how deep the wounds of such experiences go.

How can we help each other heal these wounds? As victims of abuse, we must allow the wound to scar, or we will always remain imprisoned in the past. An open wound makes it impossible to move forward. Each of us can influence our own psychological well-being, though I am sometimes told I am cruel when I offer this advice. I think the cruelty lies in holding onto trauma, wallowing in it, and blaming it for everything that goes wrong in life. When we are able to face tragedy, we must learn to let it go so that we can see our way straight and move forward.

How does faith contribute to the art of letting go? What I am about to say may sound simple, and yet it can be so difficult to accomplish: we can and should learn to give all our pain and worry to God; only he can ensure we are treated justly. Jesus told us that we should forgive not only seven times but seventy times seven (see Matt. 18:22).

Contrary to what we might think, this directive does not cheapen grace. God's forgiveness reaches as far as Jesus's journey to the cross and reconciliation of the world. Aided by the light of faith, we can manage to forgive others and let go of even the most difficult burdens we've been forced to carry.

The decisive step occurs when we recognize that God has forgiven us and given his Son so that we may have eternal life, as it is written in John's Gospel (see John 3:16). This gift is one of the greatest mysteries of our faith, though many people find it difficult to understand.

Most people still recognize Jesus's existence—that he may have been God's Son and that he offered us rules to live by before dying on the cross. They might even think: *It's a shame, really; too bad it ended so badly.* But the church declares this death was for our sins. An internal response to this might be: *But why? He doesn't know me, and besides, yesterday's little white lie doesn't warrant something this drastic.* Or does it?

Fundamentally, most people regard themselves as good people who don't do anything that would fit in the momentous category of sin. If something does fit that category, they would maintain it doesn't concern Jesus, if he even existed. As for the notion of resurrection, well, let's just say it's an alien concept.

In what follows, let's examine the Resurrection more closely.

Comfort and Hope

Many texts summarized in the Bible are considerably older than the traditions of Christianity. The authenticity of these older sources is generally more recognized than the legitimacy of the Bible itself, and yet these texts serve to confirm the Bible's trustworthiness. Historically, scholars confirm that Jesus lived and died by crucifixion. Many witnesses gave testimony of his resurrection; they saw him and testified that he spoke with them.

This Jesus of Nazareth declares that he rose from the dead, and we can too. At what point do we object? When does it become too much to believe? The sacred texts suggest that one follows from the other—to experience Christ's resurrection is to anticipate our own.

Jesus did not merely talk about this mystery. He let his actions confirm his words. When he appeared to his disciples after the resurrection, he allowed Thomas—doubting Thomas—to touch his wounds. Consider the way this teaching gives validity to the Christian faith, offering a powerful perspective of the resurrection life beyond death.

I yearn for people to sense the power of the Resurrection in their lives and often ask myself how I can break apart this nourishing loaf of bread so that it can be understood and received by others.

There are theologians among us who deny the Resurrection altogether. They refute the so-called "substitutionary atonement" doctrine with its language of sacrifice. They oppose the notion that Jesus had to offer his life for us before God because it is simply too cruel to accept. I agree that Christ's death was cruel, but the consequences of sin are just as cruel and burdensome.

In light of this teaching, do you understand how far God's love can go?

If we don't believe in the Resurrection, we can forget everything else. Jesus's death would have been completely in vain, rendering absurd all that he'd said and done before.

Thankfully, Jesus did rise from the dead and through his death enables us to rid ourselves of sin in the presence of our forgiving God. I must recognize, in every circumstance and way, that he also died for *my* sins, for those I commit *today*.

Let's take another look at what we might consider an antiquated term—sin. Imagining the world from the vantage point of one of Jesus's contemporaries might be helpful, such as one of the soldiers following orders at the Crucifixion. Maybe I would have been like the disciples who ran away when the going got tough. If Jesus were alive today my sin would be just as great, and for that very reason I would want to follow him.

I think we have not adequately acknowledged the fact that the disciples ran away. Jesus's arrest and death signaled the collapse of the way they made sense of the world. Their despair over the meaninglessness of his death must have felt abysmal. I recognize this feeling from people with a serious illness. But another response to imminent death is possible. An acquaintance of mine who was seriously ill with cancer came to look upon the crucified Christ with deeper understanding. She carried within herself the sure knowledge that she would make it through her final days because of her faith in the Resurrection. She simply claimed Jesus's resurrection for herself, as the apostle Paul wrote in his letter to the Romans: "Therefore we have been buried with him by baptism into death, so that, just as Christ was raised from the dead by the glory of the Father, so we too might walk in newness of life" (Rom. 6:4). Consider how much calmer we might be as we journey with confidence through suffering and death!

Did Jesus know that he would rise after three days? Yes, and no. As God's Son, he knew the promises of the Old Testament, but we are also familiar with his anguished prayer in the Garden of Gethsemane. He asked his father to let this "cup" pass him by. And recall his cry from the cross: "My God, my God, why have you forsaken me?" (Mk. 15:34). Jesus knew this cry of profound loneliness from an ancient Psalm of David (see Ps. 22:1).

Jesus is not an aloof deity who can face his suffering and death because he knows he'll come back to life in three days. Because he knew the anguish of death, he can be profoundly present to us in our own loneliness and fear.

No, his death was not in vain; nor was it a tragic mistake. Christ's death and resurrection are the most important events in the history of the world. Our life and our suffering need not be in vain. For this reason, we should not turn and run like the disciples when we face hardships. They were driven by a lack of understanding, by fear and despair over what they understood to be the meaninglessness of Jesus's death. Today we may be tempted to turn from God because faith appears to be superfluous. As our churches become emptier, we may not experience the relevance of worship as people did in earlier ages. When I hear such excuses, I want to shout out: "Look at the fire and not the ashes! Don't turn away from this gift!"

Instead, we seem to repress our faith and ignore this gift in our lives. In light of this travesty, I find it increasingly difficult to conduct traditional funeral rites. I know of a pilot who left the church some years ago, insisting that he be cremated when he died so that his ashes could be spread from an airplane over Italy. I believe we lose a part of our capacity to remember when we reject the church's ancient burial rites. Cemeteries used to be reminders that life is fragile and passing. But today people want all traces of their lives erased. I would implore such people not to take memorial spaces away from the people who love them. These places offer some consolation and rest for their grief.

To a certain extent, we enter eternity each time we go to a cemetery. It is where we are placed for our final rest—or, as we say in German, where we "make our final bed." Cemeteries can put the hectic pace of our lives in proper perspective because they allow us to feel connected with something larger than ourselves.

At the Threshold to Eternity

Many people argue in favor of assisted suicide as a release from their suffering and a way to end life on their own terms. Such an idea evokes a troubling question: Isn't this kind of thinking shortsighted? Yet without hope in the Resurrection, some people might feel trapped in their own cottages of existence. It's no wonder people tell themselves: "I'm tired of living with my loneliness and pain; my life is pointless. I'd rather put an end to it all."

In the face of certain and painful death, many people would prefer to receive a lethal injection. What is actually going on inside a person who experiences constant pain and has become tired of living? How can I open another reality to such a person?

I'd like to tell them: "You're still full of life *now*. The top of the hourglass may be running out, but the bottom is full. Your life hasn't dissipated into the abyss; experience this last phase consciously, learn what it has to teach, and know that beyond this life the best is yet to come!"

Some people have the opposite attitude and cling to life at all costs. They are unable to let go because they think this world contains the whole of their existence. With its hope in the Resurrection, the Christian faith is the greatest source of help for them too!

A man told me a story that illustrates the good that can come from the events surrounding death. His father-in-law suddenly had to undergo a difficult operation. When the man saw him after surgery, he was all but convinced that his father-in-law wouldn't make it, but he ended up living for another six months. In retrospect, this man came to regard the illness of his father-in-law as a gift for the family, since it allowed them to adjust to the notion of his death and gave them the opportunity to say goodbye. At first, they were convinced the medical apparatus was the only thing keeping his father-in-law alive. How powerless the man had felt! All that seemed to be left of his father-in-law was the shell of a body attached to a machine, unable to speak or communicate. This kind of helplessness makes us conscious of our own finitude and fragility, though a proper awareness of the reality of death might bring us back to our senses.

The father-in-law had never been a man of faith, but one evening that changed. It became clear why this time of suffering had been necessary, and the son-in-law experienced a greater closeness with his father-in-law than he had ever known.

The younger man spent a long time simply sitting by the bed because the ill man could hardly speak. He finally asked, "Is there anything I can do for you?"

His father-in-law answered, "You can pray to your God for me."

He began by praying freely and concluded with the Our Father. After a moment of silence, the father-in-law sighed deeply and said, "That felt so good!"

That's all he said; nothing more was needed to suggest how deeply his father-in-law had felt spoken to and reached by God.

The depth of this encounter would have been impossible without the suffering that preceded it. Such experiences can strengthen us in dealing with the pain in our lives. Many others beyond the family circle benefited from this man's experience because the son-in-law spoke about it at the funeral. We don't know whether others are able to make peace with God in the final stretch of their life's journey or whether they simply sense the presence of a God who loves them. We're not in a position to judge. This is a matter decided between God and each of us at the time of our death.

I regard this man's experience as a sign of his deep and unspoken longing for faith, though it may have been buried under the distractions of life's pressures. He may not have wanted to believe until he could discover God in his own way, and yet he seemed to find real comfort late in his life. Where do these barriers come from? For some people, the pastor of their youth may have rendered the idea of access to God impossible. Others may have experienced terrible abuse, as we have witnessed in the Catholic Church. These experiences certainly have the potential to leave us disillusioned by others and let down by God.

The story of this man shows that even if we find no need to live by faith in God until the end of our life, faith can still comfort us and help us undergo death. If such deep experiences of renewal and consolation are possible, it seems a pity to wait so long to encounter God.

The longing for a God who offers safety and comfort can be different from the ideas often communicated about God. Many people assume that God is narrow-minded and unimaginative because of their own distorted images. Because we consider ourselves independently minded and capable of great responsibility, we may not take kindly to the notion of a God who comforts us. Too many ideas about God, however, have absolutely nothing to do with his true nature, which is why I long to tell people about the benevolent God I have come to know during the course of my life.

Unanticipated Possibilities

Jesus's central command is nothing more and nothing less than to love God and our neighbor with all our heart. With God present in our lives we find love, healing, generosity, and new birth—a powerful experience mirrored in our encounters with others.

That's exactly what happened in the hospital between this dying man and his son-in-law. Even if the son-in-law would never have called what he did pastoral ministry, he cared for the soul of another, bringing his father-in-law's soul up from the cellar of despair and into the warming light of God's presence. A deep connection was formed between them, and the son-in-law spoke of how he could finally encounter his father-in-law with love in the context of his life, even though they had often disagreed in the past.

In situations such as these, something often breaks open between two people; hardened boundaries loosen, and new possibilities emerge when God is present.

The transmission of faith does not belong to the domain of the ordained alone. Authenticity and honesty are crucial; we should share only those things we can stand behind in faith.

Many people ask me how I live my faith in concrete terms, and they seem to want to know the truth about my life. Such a conversation would be over the moment they had the sense I was faking it, pretending to believe something that I did not and thus holding to a faith that was nothing more than an existential lie. Faith can't simply gloss over what doesn't make sense to us. Faith offers us guidance precisely so that we don't have to build our lives upon lies.

At some point, nearly everyone wants help navigating the question of God. This moment of truth happens for some people on their deathbed. For others like me, it can happen at age fourteen, the time in my life when I made the firm decision to follow a spiritual path and enter monastic life.

Only in the face of suffering and death do we recognize that the question "Why should I believe?" is insufficient because it leaves us with nothing to do. The better question might be "Why am I allowed to believe?" because it expresses the truth that faith is a great opportunity.

This opportunity shows up repeatedly in our lives. Following any tragedy people look for and find comfort in God amidst the community that mourns with them. Whether in the case of an accident or a suicide, faith can immerse us in a helpful and life-giving ritual. Others may come to understand how faith opens up the possibility of seeing things in a different light. In the face of death we often find ourselves asking, "What is it exactly that makes life meaningful?"

Some people try to avoid such questions by saying: "Life is unfair; it was just bad luck. Life ends for all of us in one way or another." Others dismiss the sting of death with a superficial spiritual response, saying something like: "It's not all that tragic. At least they'll live on elsewhere." Anyone who can take the loss of another human being so lightly has probably never experienced a deep relationship or shown any real interest in other people.

Those who can feel pain and loss are certainly healthier. I tell them God is real; he feels their pain and stands alongside them. Jesus's promise—"I am the way, the truth, and the life"—offers real comfort (John 14:6). It is a way to say, "You don't walk this journey of pain alone!" On this journey, some people experience the cross as a sign of hope; they know that death is not the end. They realize that despite the goodness of life the best is yet to come. Death doesn't have to be the end for us or for those we love. We need to allow this great hope to offer us deep and true comfort.

My goal for this first part of the book was to provide good reasons why we can and should believe in God. We will approach the practicalities of belief in the second part by asking the question: "How then do we believe?"

faith—how does that work?

Trust

Many people have no idea how to draw closer to God. What are the first steps?

Simply put, faith means trust. We make no progress in faith without a certain childlike trust that there is someone to whom we pray. This childlike posture is one of humility, an indivisible dimension of faith.

But this notion has become suspect in our day. Too often we equate humility with holding ourselves back, and many of us—particularly those who see themselves as movers and shakers—have difficulty with this notion. I often find myself wondering how to speak of such matters to leaders in our society. Does such an emphasis seem soft and ineffective?

In the course of my work I often find myself speaking to audiences that include hard-driving business managers and blue-collar union workers. Many of these people have little interest in matters of faith, which causes me to wonder why I'm invited to address them in the first place. But such people still experience a real yearning for something more in their lives, and some of them are committed persons of faith.

Among them I think of Alfred Herrhausen, a banker and devoted Christian who was assassinated in 1989, apparently because of his work involving the pardoning of debt for nations in the developing world. Former General Secretary of the United Nations, Dag Hammarskjöld, lived out his convictions by faithfully taking responsibility for the well-being of others. The late Norbert Walter, for many years the chief economist of Deutsche

Bank, was a profoundly engaged Christian and a leader of his local congregation.

Many of us must learn to grow in faith by moving beyond the piety of our childhood toward a properly engaged and responsible relationship with God. We needn't presume tension or contradiction exists between these stages of faith; such development is natural, and each Christian must find their unique path. But the journey always begins with trust.

Let's assume you've decided to take the first steps of faith, or you've already begun the journey. That means you're ready to give yourself over to the possibility of more than what you've already thought or experienced. What's next?

When you've decided to allow your life to be shaped by faith—for the first time or in a renewed way—I would warn you against making the common mistake of turning first to the church's teaching. Rather than taking up catechism or delving into some other way of knowing *about* God, focus on a personal relationship *between* you and God. Only after you've given yourself to God in a personal way should you turn to instruction, making it possible to understand from an entirely new orientation.

How then do we begin to establish a personal relationship with God?

Opening Ourselves Anew

We're often afraid of simply letting go and giving ourselves to a real conversation with God, which has much to do with our false images of God. When someone wants to return to the church, their initial fear involves what the church might ask of them financially, such as a tithe. This obstacle saddens me, particularly since it reflects a distorted image that obstructs our path forward in our relationship with God. Many of us live with inherited notions of God that are boring in the best case and downright repressive in the worst—as if God wants to deny us pleasure, even to the point of instilling fear within us. Such twisted images of God prevent us from finding our way to the true path of faith.

In such situations, encountering other faithful Christians can bring great encouragement. We need to intentionally seek out community with other Christians; involvement in congregational life can be a source of joy.

We can also draw on the experiences of faith we had as children. Children naturally experience God's presence in a simple and beautiful way. In the context of a healthy relationship, they trust their mothers and fathers. A mother can say, "God is truly present to you, just as your father and I are here for you." Such a simple affirmation can be instructive, enabling children to progress step by step in faith. Eventually their relationship with God will deepen through religious instruction and the experience of public worship with fellow Christians.

Our faith is often tested for the first time when we reach puberty, in part because of the enormous role sexuality begins to play in our lives. If we've grown up with the impression that God wants to prohibit us from enjoying the world and each other, we might find ourselves distancing ourselves from such a God. Healthy sexual development is as important as healthy spiritual or religious formation. In the course of our religious upbringing, it is crucial for us to experience an attitude that recognizes that God created sexuality and finds it good, but also that the expression of our sexuality is only one part of our experience. Our coming-of-age ought to help us see that we should do what brings us joy and experience our passions as they come. Faith in God will offer guidance; his ways and means will prevent us from hurting ourselves and others.

I'm amazed by how much negativity permeates the ways we experience our sexuality. The experience of freedom in sexuality does not necessarily lead us to a holistic experience of sex. Love is the highest aim here! This claim opposes the widespread belief in the individual will and presumes that giving ourselves over to our feelings, passions, and dreams will inevitably lead to healthy self-realization, which is rarely the case.

Whatever our experiences might have been, we can still turn our lives toward this path of trust, even if initially we can take only small steps. It might be time to stop and consider: "What I am really doing here? Where do I want to go? Can this be all there is?"

The Blessing of Sundays

Attending worship offers us the opportunity to find ourselves and learn to listen to our own experience. In our culture, men are far less visible in the church than women. Though worship often seems downright suspect from a certain perspective, we might discover that faith offers a deep sense of orientation that allows us to open our hearts—if only we can slow down like the hamster stepping off the spinning wheel in its cage!

Sunday worship is important, though not necessarily as a ritual we dutifully keep. Such an attitude does not sufficiently address our fundamental needs as human beings. Consider what it might mean to approach Sunday as a day set aside for quiet and meditation, initiating a sense of celebration and personal formation.

Sunday can be a day when we pull back from the activity of our lives in order to remember that we are not simply functional beings. God sets aside the Sabbath as a day of rest, marking it as one of the Ten Commandments in order to demonstrate its importance.

Sunday is often the only day in the week when we are not driven by appointments, a day when we can find our way to a sense of quiet. In this sense, the obligation we feel to attend worship can be experienced as an unwelcome duty, prompting us to look for a different day to attend church. Many congregations offer opportunities for evening worship after work on other days of the week, but Sunday is the day set aside for celebration, the day of faith in the congregation's life.

I am suggesting we each need to set aside a day for true worship, one that is celebrative and offers the strength and quiet we need in our lives. If we give ourselves to the task of searching for such an experience, we will find opportunities that guide us to an ever deeper experience of God.

Our Own Experience—Priceless!

Now let us consider how we can cultivate our own experiences, which can unfold in many different ways.

Much help can be found in the monastic tradition: opportunities to encounter quiet at regular intervals during each day, experience ritual, and participate in a community of stillness and attentiveness. But how can we find these experiences in our daily lives outside of the monastery?

This question can only be answered by those who first visit our monasteries and walk a part of the journey with us. I can only discover the beauty in Mozart's *Coronation Mass* by listening to it; only when I've experienced it can I be thrilled by it. The same is true for other music. Only when we've taken music into our very being are we truly able to inhabit it and introduce others to its gift.

I am regularly amazed when I visit the school we run in the monastery at St. Ottilien and experience its orchestra firsthand.

I find the young people who take up an instrument as difficult as the violin and practice diligently for years in order to master it impressive. When we approach an endeavor in the proper manner, nothing is too difficult to achieve.

It is worth remembering to tell ourselves and others to just get started! When we're finally underway, let us learn to pay attention to our experience.

One doesn't learn how to play soccer by being a spectator or watching games on television, and reading a book is of limited value in our attempt to master it. If we are truly fascinated with the sport, we must devote time to developing our skills on the field, smelling the grass, and playing the game for its own delight.

Even reading this book can only give you a dim sense of what I mean when I say that I am truly in love with God because of the path I have chosen. In this sense, the church is like a stadium, and the fragrance of incense and candles corresponds to the smell of grass on the soccer field. The crowd joining to cheer for a goal is similar to the shared experiences we find in the community of faith. When we score our first goal, we find God's presence on our particular path in life.

How do we get to this point? By thinking it through logically? We rely primarily on reason in our intellectual lives. We presume that everything must be systematically explicable in order for us to accept it, but this is only one possibility. The most unassailable argument is and remains our personal experience.

At the moment I find myself gazing out of my study window in Rome. I see the amazing colors of the sunset cast on the nearby buildings. While I can attempt to describe this with eloquence, someone who has never been here can hardly begin to imagine this particular beauty. Only those who have seen and experienced it are in a position to understand what I mean when I describe it.

Helpful Companions for the Journey

While our experience of faith is personal, conversations with other Christians can offer great help on this path and answer many of our questions.

In the beginning, much about the life of faith will seem strange. A man once told me about his visit to a particular art exhibit that took place every five years. He had no great appreciation of art, but he met someone with considerable knowledge about such matters. As he described this encounter, he spoke of the way his own horizon extended beyond anything he could have anticipated. Although he had once stood before these same pieces and found some to be quite nice, others a bit strange, and many completely incomprehensible, his perspective changed as his guide explained one piece after another. In this manner, he found himself beginning to understand these works of art.

Our experience of faith is much the same. We have to live our own experiences and go our own way, but it is extremely important to realize that we do not have to travel this path alone. We need to search out helpful companions for our journey. Consider carefully who might serve this purpose. A priest or minister isn't necessarily required to explain such matters.

Who strikes you as a person capable of attending to such questions? Who impresses you with their authenticity? Seek out people who express curiosity without needing to have an answer for every question, those who are willing and able to engage you in a whole-hearted manner. When you find such a person, go alongside them on the way.

Getting Started

One of the benefits that comes from seeking to live a Christian life is that we no longer view the other as a competitor; moving up or down becomes irrelevant as we begin to see with the loving eyes of God. Certainly aggression and the widespread unhappiness in our world would begin to decline if more people thought and acted in this manner.

To be bent low to the ground and racked with fear ennobles no one, but people flourish when they encounter trust and love.

Orienting our lives with regard to the carpenter's son from Nazareth is a true way. Again we recall Jesus's words: "I am the way, the truth, and the life" (John 14:6). We can learn much from Jesus as we walk this path. He often repeated the invitation "Follow me!" Regrettably, these words have come to sound unappealing because Jesus walked the path of sacrifice all the way to the cross. While many among us are understandably wary, Jesus's way of self-renunciation is essentially a deep love for others. In the same way that Jesus did, we can practice turning away from our preoccupation with ourselves so that we can encounter the totality of each other.

How do I explain what it means to "follow me"?

A mother understands this better than most, especially if she has raised many children. She no longer thinks of herself first but is happy when her children thrive. When I speak with her about God's love for people, we have a shared understanding because she practices a form of selfless love every day toward her children and family. She has experienced the way of God and fundamentally understands much about Jesus's teaching.

For those who work in the business world, this concept looks quite different and may not seem so simple. They must focus on profit and pay attention to keeping the upper hand. In such a context, a selfless attitude is especially demanding. Such people also have a life outside of their work.

I am not opposed to making money, as long as those engaged in business maintain the capacity to think beyond the realm in which they work—and I am not referring to hobbies or luxurious amenities. Such things are to be enjoyed, and I don't wish to deny people the pleasure of them. Money can bring about great good, but if we imagine that having money will bring happiness, we are deceived. That said, people who are wealthy can follow in the way of Jesus insofar as they model their lives on his.

The real problem is deeper. Those who are self-employed or working in the business world walk a difficult path because they must devote ten to twelve hours each day to their work, which demands a considerable expenditure of energy. When it comes to taking time in the evening for God, we can be completely exhausted after a tough day of work, wanting only to put up our feet and relax. God comes to us in these times and says, "You're working too hard, and you recognize in the depths of your heart that there is no time left for you or for us together."

On the basis of conversations I've had over the years, I know many people acutely feel this challenge. They are troubled in the depths of their heart. They want more room in their lives for what's important and desire to find meaning by sorting out the question of God for themselves. To recognize and turn our attention is a step in the right direction.

Creating Open Spaces in Our Lives

Let's assume that you sense such an interest, perhaps even a yearning, to become more intimately acquainted with God. In the same way we experience human relationships, the first step is close at hand: we must set aside time for the person we want to know, and for this we must create spaces in our life. We may need to learn to say no more often—particularly in the workplace—despite others' and even our own demands and expectations.

We want to be so many things—successful, attractive, physically fit, a caring parent, an esteemed colleague. The desire to excel in everything thrusts us into a breathless tempo that will eventually, and quite literally, rob us of our breath altogether.

We need to take small steps. They show us how to bring our life into proper balance again. When a busy person is able to observe a proper Sunday Sabbath, he has already staked out a claim for finding stability and creating space in which to engage God.

What helps us keep God before us in the midst of our busy lives? Beyond the need to establish and maintain proper balance, only one thing will suffice:

We must accept the fact that absolute perfection does not exist in this world, no matter how we may try to live as though it does.

We must accept the fact that we will fail at many things, that mistakes are inevitable even when we try to avoid them. If we seek to live a perfect life, to attain the highest degree of accomplishment in every aspect of our lives, we will create great stress for ourselves and those around us. Neither our children nor our partners or colleagues are able to satisfy such demands.

The Rule of St. Benedict offers great help in this regard: the abbot should not be "excitable, anxious, extreme, obstinate, jealous, or over suspicious. Such a man is never at rest. Instead, he must show forethought and consideration in his orders, and whether the task he assigns concerns God or the world, he should be discerning and moderate" (RB 64.16–17).

Practical Faith

Finding a God-pleasing path does not require following a precise set of instructions, but we ought to consider carefully what shape such a life takes. The Bible contains a wealth of practical advice, and the psalmist addresses the question by describing what a person of faith looks like:

> LORD, *who may abide in your tent?*
>   *Who may dwell on your holy hill?*
>
> *Those who walk blamelessly and do what is right,*
>   *and speak the truth from their heart;*
> *who do not slander with their tongue,*
>   *and do no evil to their friends,*
>   *nor take up a reproach against their neighbors;*
> *in whose eyes the wicked are despised,*
>   *but who honor those who fear the LORD;*
> *who stand by their oath even to their hurt;*
> *who do not lend money at interest,*
>   *and do not take a bribe against the innocent.*
>
> *Those who do these things shall never be moved. (Psalm 15)*

No mention of pious penitential acts is made, only the way in which we interact with others. The Psalms repeatedly focus on the commandments of God, as Psalm 119 makes clear.

Such passages point to the importance of just action and compassionate care for the vulnerable—widows, the poor, the elderly, and strangers. The thrust of these Psalms points to how the divine commandments light our path and orient us on our way.

In light of this truth, I'd like to address the pressure and doubt we experience when we fail to pray or attend church.

Not everyone is called to enter a monastery. Our journey with God must simply begin where we are, in the midst of everyday life— perhaps with a small and fervent prayer or with attentive care for others.

The journey won't be easy; roads without potholes and unfamiliar terrain are rare. But this is the way God calls us forth, stirring our consciousness through the various realities of our lives. For example, you might be met with resistance when you speak with your boss about boundaries, even when the conversation is approached in a friendly but firm manner. "This way will not be an easy one," sings the German R&B artist Xavier Naidoo. But we do not journey on our path alone.

God Journeys with Us

Even in the church we do not walk alone. Though we stumble into doubt, the good Lord can work—give him room! Of course, we are still called to do our part. For example, the current trend in pastoral work is to emphasize the priest in charge, but to my mind this inclination reflects how many in the church have too little trust in the Spirit and in the faithful.

I am convinced that God's Spirit is working behind the scenes in the sexual abuse scandal facing the Catholic Church today in order that God's church might be cleansed. It's high time that all of this comes to light and can finally be fully dealt with! More broadly, I am certain the Spirit will do great work in our time, turning many things inside out.

Change has much less to do with us than it does with the Spirit of God.

Remembering that the Spirit works in us relieves us of the pressure that everything depends on us. The beautiful truth is that we are invited to trust in God's actions, and this divine intervention belongs to the deepest experiences of our Christian faith. Even if the world ridicules us, the truth remains: we travel no path alone.

Praying

The first and most interior form by which we live out a personal relationship with God is prayer. When we speak with another person, we experience one of the most basic forms of relationship. The same is true with God.

Many people find praying difficult. How do we to begin? What do we say? It is crucial that we learn to overcome our shyness. No particular form of prayer must be observed, though formulated prayers are fine, particularly when we simply can't find the words. Such prayers can help us make a start. But in a fundamental sense, we can speak with God just as we do with any other person—or better said, with a very good friend. We do not need to ponder what it is we want to say.

Certainly there are highly refined prayers, but these are usually responses to some particular situation in which we find ourselves. The narrow, egotistical prayers we make focus on our personal happiness. Sometimes we only have time and strength for a short, inner cry for help, but there are also sacred moments when we have the sense that God is answering our call and widening the horizon of our lives.

Many people say, "I simply can't pray; I don't know any prayers." We don't need specific prayers in order to pray. Simply speak to God. Begin in whatever manner feels natural. Besides your petitions and needs, speak with him about the things that stir you. Give voice to what is beautiful with gratitude and joy.

We often thoughtlessly exclaim, "My God!" But what would it be like to give voice to something that pleases us, saying in a simple way, "Lord God, that's beautiful!" We are sometimes so exhausted by the time evening comes a simple prayer is all we can manage. Even for highly disciplined people this can be the case. Perhaps begin by consciously reflecting back on the events of the day. You might be startled to discover many beautiful things that otherwise would have disappeared into the caverns of forgetfulness.

An acquaintance of mine once told me that this practice always evoked profound gratitude within him. As he put it, "This changes my life." A prayerful retrospection can lead to a genuine sense of gratitude, a feeling that can become a foundational melody by which we value our lives. Our way becomes easier; we might even be able to imagine flying!

Giving thanks is a basic, foundational posture by which we come to take ourselves seriously as human beings. Contrary to what we might think, it does not exclude our own reality and cares. Placing prayers of thanks alongside the ongoing prayers we utter in times of need does us a world of good.

Just as in interpersonal relationships, our relationship with God becomes increasingly intimate the more we speak with him. Over time, we acquire a deepening sense of God's presence in our daily lives.

Though it has become something of a cliché, the poem "Footprints in the Sand" comes to mind. A person looking back over his life notices footprints on a beach. Sometimes two sets are visible, sometimes only one. The second set belongs to Jesus, who had promised to accompany him. Yet at the place of his most extreme need, the person notices only a single set of footprints. He says to Jesus, "I don't understand why, when I needed you most, you would leave me"—to which Jesus replies, "When you see only one set of footprints, it was then that I carried you."

This nearness, this sense of being carried, can only be experienced when we recognize the quiet voice of God and his presence. Like any other skill, we must practice.

I'd like to encourage you to speak with God more often, whenever you find it possible. Perhaps when you're sitting at a red light or waiting at the doctor's office. Turn your thoughts toward him while standing in line at the supermarket and before you eat. The quiet moments of your life are a great place to start.

Beginning and Ending the Day with God

In my life as a monk, I experience the beneficial effects of a framework for life. Within the monastery, we observe set times for prayer each day. Perhaps an established rhythm would be helpful for you as well, such as the decision to begin and end each day with God. In time, you will find that such a pattern ushers you differently into and out of the day, blessing your sleep.

Morning prayer has the advantage of giving me a purpose at the very start of the day: I find myself speaking with someone. I'm something of a grouse in the mornings, but this practice brings me out of myself into a larger relationship with life. In earlier days of monastic life, we were wakened in our rooms as a senior monk sang in Latin, *Benedicamus domino*—"Let us bless the Lord." We answered, *Deo gratias. Laudetur in aeternum. Amen*—which is to say, "Thanks be to God, who is to be praised unto eternity."

I continue to observe this tradition each morning, regardless of where I am. In my sleepiness, this practice conveys a thought that extends beyond me and my particular condition, one that relativizes my cares and concerns and reminds me, *You are not bound by the tasks of the day; something greater rises above them.*

In contrast to many of the invitations we hear to practice meditation, we are not so concerned with questions like: "How's it going for you? How was your sleep? How do you feel today?" Instead, I am able to rise up through the conditions and circumstances of life and bring them into proper proportion. Of course, I'm not always doing well when I wake up, but is that really so important?

If I've not slept well on a given night, nothing more has happened than the fact that I didn't sleep well. That's part of life, though my troubled sleep might serve as an indication of the demands I place on myself. It doesn't always have to be a matter of great importance.

When I prepare myself for the coming day, this glance to the heavens can be a great help. Of course I want to work effectively, fulfill my responsibilities faithfully, and make progress on the projects before me. But we should not make a god of our work. Orienting myself toward God early in the morning helps me live my day differently than I might otherwise—whether it be an ordinary day or a day when I am to make an important presentation, engage in a significant conversation, or offer spiritual direction to someone who comes to me.

I enter into each conversation and important engagement with a short prayer: "God, let me say and do the right thing, and give me your Spirit." In doing so, a different atmosphere is created. Prayer is not about obtaining a guarantee; it may well be that God desires something other than I intend. Rather, prayer prepares me differently, relativizing the whole, freeing me a little from my own intentions and interests. My way becomes real, true, and authentic. Yes, I believe God works in everyday experiences, which is a relief to me when I face difficult conversations because I am not a trained therapist, and I regularly find myself confronting my limitations. But I trust that God can handle these limitations and overcome them. In spiritual direction sessions, I am sometimes perfectly equipped for the moment, but if the other person is not open, I cannot make anything happen simply on the strength of my professional competence.

A CEO of a large company once told me that his secretary often prayed when he was facing difficult discussions or needed to offer leadership in particular situations. He experienced working in this atmosphere as a great gift, thankful that someone knew the demands he faced and supported him in the work he needed to accomplish. More was at stake than simply accomplishing his own interests. Rather than praying for a particular outcome, one prays that God's will be done; it can be a great help to remember that God is present, revealing his own purposes and intentions. The goal is not to accomplish one thing or another but rather to have a conversation about the process at hand. Behind such an attitude we can sense great trust in God's leading.

This trust can give rise to a freedom of purpose in which we discover that everything and everyone are not pressuring us. It's something like when others ask me, "Why do Benedictines exist?" My answer is always the same: "For nothing, really, other than living and singing our praises to God." I often add: "For this reason we're open to all sorts of work. But we weren't made for some particular purpose."

In the company I just spoke about, a short, quarter-hour meditation and a prayer group take place. Both activities are considered part of the workday, and while some people might consider these interruptions a way to get more overtime hours, these undertakings are an invaluable part of a larger company culture—one that can't be measured in terms of productivity but rather in terms of shared sympathies, attention, and connection.

A movement in Chile has spawned three great schools that observe daily *lectio divina* (divine reading). The teachers pray the daily scriptural readings together with their students. At noon each day, they come together for conversation, and in the evening before they leave for home, they engage in a discussion of passages from the Scriptures. I am convinced this practice establishes a much different atmosphere than most schools maintain these days. Rather than trying to assert authority, teachers and students operate within a dialogue—with the Bible, with God, and with each other.

Imagine what it might be like if such an approach, embraced by more people in authentic and modest ways, began to shape companies and schools? By engaging each other differently, we might come to experience the strength of faith in our culture. We could revolutionize our entire society!

We should not, therefore, limit ourselves to morning and evening prayer, but we should also not overwhelm ourselves. A small prayer every so often throughout the day is wonderful. It isn't necessary to always consider the matter of time, saying to ourselves, *I need a quarter-hour to pray, and there's so much I need to do. . . .*

Faith depends on a lively relationship, not the fulfillment of duty. We are not required to pray; we are allowed to do so. Prayer should not burden us; prayer frees us.

In an earlier age, it seemed natural to pray in the middle of each day. We prayed to "the angel of the Lord" three times during the day. While only a short prayer, it enabled us to glance in God's direction, encouraging and giving us the strength to continue on. At noon the church bells would ring, reminding farmers to pause in their fields to pray.

I know a very busy monk who was asked how he could meet the burdens of his daily obligation to pray, particularly because he was constantly interrupted. His response was direct: "I accomplish all this work *because* I have these times set aside for prayer. They help me to concentrate my mind when I am working, but they also assist in keeping me from being overwhelmed by my work."

When I feel pressured by my morning work, midday prayers quiet me, and I experience something that seems like redemption. How could I manage otherwise? So many of us start early and find ourselves overwhelmed by the needs at hand. At times we are ready to collapse with exhaustion, so we pause to eat something or drink another cup of coffee—and thus our life goes on. How beneficial it would be to find a different rhythm to live by, one that takes the wholeness of life into consideration!

The spiritual life is shaped by such a rhythm. It is a good thing to develop a cadence of prayer in our life with God. Ideally, a balanced sequence of prayer, work, and study would be wonderful. Our lives as Benedictines are summed up in a similar way: to "pray and work and read" (*ora et labora et lege*).

Finding Our Own Rhythm

Ora et labora et lege gives me a certain distance from the things I am engaged in doing. Prayer keeps me connected to what is real. It reminds me that work is not the only important thing in my life. While work remains significant, it is relativized and acquires its proper worth. The reading of good books and the Bible brings inspiration and orientation.

Viewed from a purely psychological perspective, such a rhythm enables me to see things in a new way. By anchoring myself in my true being, I clarify where I've come from and what my inner existence means. In quiet security I find my God—from whom I have come and with whom I journey.

Many people who are constantly busy think that prayer is only something to grasp in times of need, but prayer is a matter of our daily, normal conversation with God.

Many people imagine that praying means lingering with God. I don't just linger with God now and then; I am always with God. In the past, this sentiment was often expressed in blunt terms. In the bathrooms and toilets of some Italian monasteries, plaques were hung that declared, "God is watching you."

And so he is. God sees us in every situation—both in times when we shine and in circumstances we'd rather hide from others. His presence is not a tool of control but rather an instrument of support. Quite simply, God is always with us. This realization can instill a deep trust similar to the kind children feel in the presence of their mother.

When facing the yearning for inner solitude and the hope of establishing proper distance from their work, many people despair that they will never be finished. I truly understand this dilemma. In such times, it helps me to keep in touch with God. When I pause to take a deep breath and pray in God's presence, I rediscover the art of anchoring myself in the midst of my activities, which gives me the quiet I need.

No Time?

Ora et labora et lege—pray, work, and read—is quite possible, though it often provokes resistance. We may think we don't have the time for such a dedicated approach. Let's consider this assumption more closely to better understand what we actually do with our time and the ways in which we fill it.

In our day, reading has been largely replaced with watching screens, particularly in the case of children and young people. However, when children find themselves on a vacation without access to television or the Internet, it is fascinating to witness the joy they find in being resourceful and finding alternative activities.

In a recent study conference held in Dillingen, Germany, the prefects focused specifically on the question of regulating television viewing and came to the conclusion that children spend far more time watching television on the weekends than during the rest of the week. When they shared this finding with parents, one father responded with complete honesty: "But what else should we do with our children?"

How startling to hear a father respond in such a way! Such an answer points to our own desire for comfort. Though we sometimes cast them aside, children are actually quite easy to engage. Too often we occupy babies with pacifiers, replacing them with computers as they grow older.

If we're entirely honest, it's not that different with adults. I am repeatedly amazed to hear how much time the average adult spends in front of screens. Without getting into a discussion of the psychological damage this can cause, we can acknowledge that interacting with screens consumes an immense amount of our free time. One also wonders what real good there is in watching television. Images crowd our minds with little benefit to our ways of thinking or the peace of our souls.

While on vacation we often discover, with some amazement, that despite missing the evening news and the happenings in our hometown, the world somehow manages to go on without us. When we return home and read through three weeks of accumulated newspapers, it becomes clear that we didn't miss much. We might even be thankful to have altogether avoided the many contentious debates among our government leaders.

Of course sometimes we simply want to relax and watching an episode of *CSI* might help. I don't necessarily have an argument against this, but I am certain we can find more beautiful ways to fill our minds and time.

It would be better to end the day with a ritual. My preference is to pray Compline, the setting for evening prayer. This text includes marvelous prayers that are genuinely helpful in finding quiet at the day's close.

Contemplation

I also find it helpful to linger without purpose in contemplation with God. Simply giving myself over to God can be a powerful experience. A similar thing happens when I pray the Psalter. As I make a psalm present in my mind, it becomes like a poem. Because I already know the words of the psalm, I can allow a particular image or a whole series of images to open themselves within me. It is the same when I pray the Rosary. In my car I always keep a CD that includes the three classic Rosary prayers and listen to them repeatedly. The practice gifts me with a deep sense of quiet, and my prayer with God is transformed into contemplation.

I cannot will this to happen or conjure it like some magic trick. A good Zen monk knows that he cannot create illumination but can only ready himself and hope that it eventually comes to him. All sorts of situations can be an opportunity for contemplation, even quite ordinary and "un-pious" activities like a visit to the toilet.

I could write another book on the ways we come in touch with God, but here I simply want to make clear that the possibilities are more than we can imagine.

This is not to say that we come into God's presence with the touch of a button. God's presence is a matter of grace.

When you sense a yearning for God, I encourage you to give yourself over expectantly to the feeling. Perhaps you will be led to spend several days as a guest in a monastery in order to find your way to others who are similarly inclined and open to sharing their experiences—people of deep quiet and peace, full of God's presence.

There are as many ways to converse with God as there are with other people. The most important condition is simply to begin.

Reading Scripture

Beautiful images continually come to me when I read. In recent days, I've been reading a real page-turner about the abbey at Cluny in France that has inspired me to think about how other abbots do their job. The book certainly removes the polished shine people often attribute to monasteries. I am often drawn to books that focus on historical subjects.

I also enjoy reading books with a practical orientation, something that shapes my own writing. My book, *Indulge in Time*, has received a very positive response precisely because of this practical focus.

People have different reading interests at different times in their lives. Many young people are fascinated by the *Harry Potter* series, which is wonderful because it brings them to reading. Reading thrillers on vacation can be fun and entertaining. I'm always amazed by how many people read on planes, and I don't quite buy the lament concerning the demise of reading in our culture. Seeing the consumption of weighty volumes, like those of Stephen King, the master of suspense and terror, always surprises me to the point of fear. Many good novels grab our attention, and even historical biographies can be exciting, introducing such personalities as Napoleon or Frederick Barbarossa.

In my life as a monk I have come to experience the act of reading as a vital part of my spiritual edification—particularly when I fill myself with something good, something that draws me toward living a successful life. It's similar to maintaining a healthy diet.

The most fascinating reading in my life continues to be the Bible. To my mind, it is rightly called "the Book of books."

When we read the Scriptures, a commentary is useful to keep at hand. Though we can certainly just dig in and start reading, many questions are likely to emerge, particularly if we begin with the Old Testament. To speak from my own experience, I always read the Bible with the assistance of a commentary in order to better grasp the cultural location and historical circumstances of the stories.

In the New Testament, I find that many people prefer to read the Gospel of John. It's certainly the best place to start, but beginning with Matthew and reading straight through is also good. Though these texts are more comprehensible than those of the Old Testament, I still read them with the assistance of a commentary.

Consider the Sermon on the Mount. How does Luke render this great passage? What of Matthew? What do these two very different versions tell us about Jesus's teaching?

My favorite time for reading is in the afternoon after a short nap. I don't usually read the Bible for a long time; a few lines suffice. Of course, one often stumbles into texts that offer more questions than answers, such as those that address homosexuality or the role of women. What is one to do with such passages?

Reading the Scriptures alongside a good commentary reminds me that such texts are always situated within a particular historical context. If I want to understand a passage rightly, I can't remove a given text from the context in which it took shape. Being faithful to the letter of a text is not enough. We must come to understand what the message of Jesus meant for the people of his time. What did they find important in his teachings?

If I really want to understand such passages, I need explanations from someone who has an extensive knowledge of the period and has studied its manners and customs more closely than I have. Take, for instance, the wedding of Cana (see John 2). In order to understand this story we need to know what weddings in the culture of this period were like. After all, we are dealing with six hundred liters of wine! The guidance of a commentary can help us grasp what Jesus was doing and deepen our understanding. Because the Bible is more than a historical report about something that happened, we need to explore the other dimensions in such a passage. Often, we will discover something about who Jesus was, what he desired, and what the author of the Gospel wanted to say to his community by the way he told the story.

Food that Truly Satisfies

People are of quite different opinions when it comes to the miracle stories. It actually doesn't matter to me whether all of them are true or not; my faith won't be affected one way or the other. I do think it is possible that Jesus changed water into wine and trust God that it was so. What is decisive about such stories is not the miracle itself, which might actually drive readers to a questionable dependence on the miraculous. In this account, the sign that lies behind the miracle is crucial. When Jesus opens the eyes of the blind, it doesn't essentially matter whether their sight is restored by way of a medical miracle or a psychological liberation. Either way, Jesus's act allows them to recognize the truth of their lives, the beauty of creation, and goodness itself.

Consider the story about the feeding of the multitudes (see Matt. 14:13–21). Why couldn't this have been possible? After all, so many things are beyond our understanding. How are we to understand phenomena like telepathy? There are times when we find ourselves thinking of someone and immediately receive an e-mail or phone call from that person without any prompting.

What am I driving at? I simply mean to say that our inability to explain something doesn't mean that it cannot be.

Ultimately, we don't need to understand everything. In the case of the feeding of the multitudes, which is told in each of the Gospels, the people received something to eat and no one seems to know how it happened. The story goes that the disciples distributed what they had without further comment. What matters is not the miracle but the truth that it illuminates:

Those who come to Jesus receive what nourishes and satisfies in abundance.

Though it might not be quite as exciting, this story could also be interpreted in terms of community. When the disciples began to distribute the food, the people brought what they had and shared it with each other. While this is a beautiful reading of the text, it does not satisfy me because I believe it is possible for God to do miracles, even when such accounts can be understood in psychological terms.

Regardless of our interpretation, the good news is the same: in the presence of God, and because of God, our hunger will be satisfied. The Bible isn't essentially about telling stories and establishing outcomes. Its purpose is to satisfy the deepest thirst we have as human beings.

Certainly many astonishing things must have happened because these stories make visible and comprehensible the remarkable person of Jesus. Nevertheless, he was never concerned simply with accomplishing miracles. We need to keep in mind that each miracle has its own meaning and purpose. When the friends of the paralytic lower him into the house where Jesus is speaking, Jesus's first word is "Son, your sins are forgiven." When the man's friends heard this, they were probably disappointed. But Jesus went on to say, "So that you may know that the Son of Man has authority on earth to forgive sins . . . I say to you, stand up, take your mat and go to your home" (Mk. 2:2–12).

If we repeatedly ask God to solve an urgent problem, and God seems to do nothing, what does that mean? Perhaps we should come to recognize that God has something else for us. Perhaps the fulfillment of our desires is not the most important thing but rather that we learn humility and let go of our pride. Perhaps an altogether different solution to our problem can be realized, one that is better than we had imagined. We often come to realize, in retrospect, that it's better things didn't happen as we'd hoped they would.

Wisdom for Life

The Bible offers many practical suggestions for living out our faith. In the Sermon on the Mount (Matt. 5–7) Jesus says much about what faith means and how it comes alive. We read about what makes us holy—which is to say, what makes us happy beyond this life—and what we can accomplish in our present lives.

The teaching in Jesus's sermon challenges us. When we read "Blessed are those who are poor in spirit, for to them belongs the Kingdom of Heaven," we are confronted with a paradox. Such a claim sets Christian faith against much of modern life; it gets under our skin and can be life-changing in ways that matter.

The Sermon on the Mount conveys practical guidance that can guide us in living our faith. Jesus tells us that righteousness, poverty, and spiritual hunger matter—qualities that develop in ordinary human situations. Those who come to understand that they can do nothing by themselves discover these teachings as offerings of hope.

In Jesus's time many people found themselves moved by his words because they could understand such images. In the Magnificat we read: "He has brought down the powerful from their thrones, and lifted up the lowly; he has filled the hungry with good things, and sent the rich away empty" (Lk. 1:52–53).

One implication we can draw from this text might be a reconsideration of our priorities. Are they properly ordered? Do we console those who are sorrowing? Are we people who do not use force, who hunger and thirst for righteousness and are thereby filled with good things?

Jesus lived in the way he describes in the Sermon on the Mount, but he is also "the way." This realization inspires me to follow him.

Purity of heart, as described in Matthew's Gospel, is also compelling. As it is written: "Blessed are those who are pure in heart, for they shall see God" (Matt. 5:8). Such purity has nothing to do with shyness but rather points to actions such as honesty, prudence, and fidelity—behaviors that come from thoroughly upright intentions. In other words, actions that we describe as authentic, that are shaped by God's trustworthiness and faithfulness.

Letting go and looking beyond ourselves entails living in a way that regards others' needs before our own. Those who no longer seek their own way will find themselves.

I am deeply moved by people who have been wealthy or successful and make a radical break in their lives, turning away from egocentric behavior and giving themselves to others. An example can be found in the tenth chapter of Mark's Gospel: "Peter began to say to him, 'Look, we have left everything and followed you.' Jesus said, 'Truly I tell you, there is no one who has left house or brothers or sisters or mother or father or children or fields, for my sake and the sake of the good news, who will not receive a hundredfold now in this age—houses, brothers and sisters, mothers and children, and fields, with persecutions—and in the age to come eternal life'" (Mk. 10:28–30).

Faith is not simply a matter of entering a place where everything will be better after we die; rather, faith makes us wealthy in the midst of our lives. Many people who don't realize this truth regard faith with indifference, which is a shame.

Lives change only when people begin to have new experiences. Reading the Bible is one such indispensable experience. Altogether too many people complain about the Bible without having actually read it. Diving in can bring rewards that surpass the pleasures of this life.

In order to engage the Bible properly, ask, "What does this mean for me?" This practice can enrich us in remarkable ways. When we find ourselves caught in the web of our own problems, as well as those of the world, we might find ourselves asking: "What can I find that is positive in this situation? How might these circumstances evoke a sense of hope?" When we continue to read and repeat his words, Jesus is able to come close.

"It will not be so among you" (Matt. 20:20) is a passage emblazoned in my mind, as well as, "Do not judge, so that you may not be judged" (Matt. 7:1).

These are profound words! I don't need to run halfway around the world in my search for meaning to find them. The wisdom for life is right here; we can read it, chew on it, and digest it. Start reading the Bible!

Together on the Way

As human beings, we are fashioned for community. In the biblical creation story, we read that it is not good for humans to be alone—a theme that we can trace all the way through the Bible. In the book of Ecclesiastes, we find the claim that "Two are better than one, because they have a good reward for their toil. For if they fall, one will lift up the other; but woe to one who is alone and falls and does not have another to help" (Eccles. 4:9–10). Recurrently we find passages in the Scriptures that bear witness to the claim that we should help one another, stand by each other, and accompany others in our lives.

Today it seems that many people live primarily for themselves, pursuing their own ends. Loneliness is a significant concern, particularly among older people.

Suppose that you intend to alter the focus of your life and place others before yourself. This way of living will not earn you more money, but it will bring a surplus of gratitude and intimacy—and thus an abundance of happiness. You will find a great return on the investment made when you give your time, heart, and attention to others.

This deep commitment to others grows naturally out of communion with God. Whenever we share with others the gift of love and strength that we receive from God, we begin to notice that our presence has a beneficial effect—just as God's presence is beneficial to us.

If we approach our life with others in this manner, we find that we don't fall so easily into the pitfalls of the helper syndrome. It is possible to deplete ourselves completely when helping others out of our own energy; in such a case, our attempts to help are no longer a healthy act of love for our neighbor. Jesus reminds us of this when he says, "Love your neighbor *as yourself*" (Mk. 12:31, emphasis added). We must fill our own reservoir in order to find the strength we need to share with others.

Many people already are a neighbor to themselves. To rephrase Jesus's command we might say: "Because you already love yourself, love your neighbor in the same way that you love yourself."

Jesus gives us another great Christian paradox when he says, "Those who lose their life . . . will find it" (see Matt. 10:39, 16:25; Mk. 8:35; Lk. 9:24). Christian faith finds its true expression and leads us to interior freedom only when we finally realize that it's not all about "me, me, me"!

Yearning for Community

We also need other people so that they can bring us along, particularly when we can't make progress on our own. We need relationships with others who can inspire and challenge us. Faith becomes easier and richer when we find ourselves with others on our journey to God.

Life in a monastery offers a particularly intimate form of such community—with many advantages and challenges. During the first several months of the monk's novitiate, everything is new and marvelous. Then, unexpectedly, people and situations begin to get on his nerves. Irritations compound: the abbot is too strict, and the monastic brothers are disorderly. The monk's vexation increases until he realizes his brothers are not perfect, relieving him of the need to be perfect himself. He discovers himself in this process, begins to doubt his own abilities, and finally comes to recognize: "My brother has found his place; I'll find mine, too. I don't have to be a know-it-all."

It takes years to discover that being part of a community is more than simply accepting others and letting them be; it means truly loving each person's individual nature, even though they may get on our nerves.

I once wrote about this in a newspaper column, and a journalist responded angrily that what I was suggesting was too much to manage—that such an expectation was unrealistic because some people are simply too difficult and unsympathetic to love. I answered her criticism by telling a story about being seated across from someone at a convention who was entirely unpleasant. I began to consider why this person was so difficult to tolerate—perhaps it was his face I didn't like. At that point I turned to God and asked, "Why have you chosen precisely this person to come into my life?" God answered, "So that your love might grow."

One of the greatest advantages of living in a community is the way we are shaped through our encounters with others and how we grow in love precisely when they get on our nerves.

My way of being with others is not perfect, as I am not perfect. I accept the fact that I cannot be everything to another person, which makes relationships easier.

I believe many marriages fail when one of the partners begins to think that the relationship must always bring absolute happiness. Limits are an essential dimension of life. People sometimes think that a monastery must be a perfect community—a misconception that leads to great disappointment when a particular weakness is revealed. In his Rule, Benedict points out that the abbot should establish life in the monastery so that the strong find what they are seeking, and the weak are not encouraged to leave. This guideline has great merit and could be applied to companies or other institutions: give the strong what they need, but don't overburden the weak.

Congregation as Community

In parishes or congregations, we are always together-on-the-way. This form of community offers a great blessing! Standing together in God's presence, joining our voices in song, and learning from other people's journeys are enriching and inspiring experiences. In many cases, this way of being together is much more helpful than a careful study of great spiritual writings carried out alone.

This community, randomly thrown together as it seems, can also be a challenge. I know people who say, "I will never extend the greeting of peace to such a motley crew!" But they voice a distorted perspective. Faith creates community and calls us, whether we like it or not, to honor others as brothers and sisters. When we do this we find that they are suddenly much closer to us than we thought.

In any given parish, it is particularly energizing to find ourselves joined in faith with others who are quite different and from many levels of society. We encounter the young together with the old. Where else do we find such an experience in today's society, except perhaps in very large extended families, which are becoming rare. Within a parish, a young mother can be encouraged by older women who have faced similar challenges in their faith. An old man can find himself enlivened by the unbridled openness and joy with which little children give themselves trustingly to God.

For this reason, I wish that children could move more freely in our congregations. In communities where their presence is viewed as a disturbance, alternate activities are often created for them. Many evangelical churches offer a concurrent worship experience geared to a child's interests and capacities. I know a Roman Catholic father who often attends such churches with his family. His children express enthusiasm about this experience because they feel that they are, quite literally, addressed in worship. The sense of community fostered in these congregations pleases children and parents alike.

Children bring a special aptitude to the work of building community. Recently, I found myself sitting in a train bound from Naples to Rome. On my left was a small child, perhaps four years old, who was looking at a book filled with illustrations of animals. He showed me each one and had me guess what kind of animal it was. Naturally, we were speaking Italian. The man sitting across from me would whisper the answers to me when I found myself stumped. By the end of the trip, a group of strangers in a train compartment were bound together in a common pursuit. A testimony to the capacity of children!

Belonging to Something Larger

Many young people attend World Youth Days and return enthusiastic and deeply moved. Such experiences of shared spiritual experience are so important for our youth and young adults. Spending time with others who are journeying in the same direction helps us understand that we are not alone in our faith journey and that we share many experiences. This is true not only in Germany but all over the world where we find others actively engaged in their relationship with Christ, part of the great family of God to which we also belong. We make new connections as our horizon expands, experiencing a feeling of belonging that many in our society yearn for.

As a missionary-Benedictine, I often find myself looking beyond the confines of my immediate environs in order to bring this message to people all around the globe. Because of this commitment, I experience a strong unity among Christians—a wonderful gift indeed.

At the present moment, many representatives of the global Benedictine community are gathering here in Rome; the first have already arrived from the United States and Australia. What a joy this is—as though we are actually brothers and sisters to each other! The issues facing Benedictines from the U.S. may be different than those facing Australians or Europeans, but amidst our differences we come together as Christians bound by a common faith. As we experience the same ideals in our minds or hearts, a particular joy is born of this experience, one that widens the boundaries of each person.

Hospitality

All people desire connection, friendship, and community—the feeling that they are welcome.

Community and hospitality are central themes for Benedictines. In 1203 Pope Innocent III made a papal visit to the newly founded monastery above Subiaco. When he discovered there was no guesthouse, he said: "But you are Benedictines, and this is a matter that ought to shape your very identity!" He gave them sufficient funds for a suitable building and provisions so that they could always receive guests.

Recently, one of the young people doing volunteer service in our community welcomed four friends who came to visit. He asked rather shyly if he could spend an afternoon together with them. When he returned in the evening, I asked him if his friends were still outside. "Yes," he said. I looked at him and said, "We have plenty to eat here; go invite them to join us!" His friends were delighted, though their initial response was to say that the invitation to dinner was not necessary and that they could go out and buy sandwiches. After coming in, they filled themselves in a way that was a joy to behold! During the meal we learned that two of the young men had been students at our school in the St. Ottilien monastery—the monastic community from which I come.

I looked at them, their plates filled to overflowing with piles of spaghetti, and found myself smiling with a deep sense of joy. Life was exactly as it should be: Christians joining together where they are, delighting in the good things of God, and sharing their experiences with each other!

Living Simply

How does one find moments of inner stillness? Not amidst the activities of daily life. At times, we must simply do nothing—a true "free" time: no radio, no music, no reading. Nothing except solitude. Such time allows us to turn from routine distractions and release the burden of our thoughts in a search for quiet.

We need time in stillness, and as we grow older this need expands. Age brings many thoughts that were not present earlier in our lives that need to be addressed. I believe that as we grow older our interior life becomes richer, but this process takes time.

I have so much to do, and at times I simply have to establish limits for my work to avoid being completely overtaken by its pressures and demands. What helps me in this endeavor? Quality rather than quantity and relationship rather than activity. I would much rather speak with you directly about this subject; writing about it in a book simply isn't possible. If we could encounter one another in person, our exchange would be enlivening.

Periods of stillness can be planned. The act of giving ourselves over to solitude requires that we let go of other things. In doing so, we discover that living a life of faith involves reducing, an experience that offers great reward.

Many people find the act of reducing to be nothing more than taking something away. But wait a moment! How do we measure such things? For some, reducing can mean letting go of the need for a third car or a twenty-five dollar bottle of wine. We might reduce the hundred pairs of shoes that fill the closet.

Seasons of fasting offer a good time to sort out such things, allowing us to see that reduction need not mean restriction. A healthy relinquishment might allow us to recognize the burdens in our lives. Setting out on a pilgrimage without heavy luggage is a beautiful experience of making do with less. Letting go enables us to experience much more of the actual person we are.

In terms of cars and other possessions, we often allow our identity to be shaped by things outside of us rather than expressed by the self within us. It would probably surprise many people to know how much joy I experience when I'm driven somewhere in a wonderful car. But I don't need it. Recently an acquaintance was raving about his Rolls Royce and wanted to give me a ride through Berlin. I'm agreeable to doing almost anything, but the experience didn't have much of an impact on me. While watching a documentary about Led Zeppelin, I was genuinely disappointed to see one of the band members driving his Rolls down the driveway of his villa. Did he really need it? In what sense was this experience fulfilling?

Such behavior often seems like an avoidance of suffering. The message appears to be: "With a mountain of money I'll be fine." The Rolling Stones exemplify this way of thinking and living; their millions seem to serve as a testimony to their happiness. But truth be told, they aren't happy, which is clear if you look carefully at their faces.

Yearning for a Simple Life

In conversations I have with a wide variety of people, I notice a genuine yearning for a simpler life, even if this desire is not acted upon. Ultimately, we come to recognize how little we actually need and that we are more than what we accumulate.

I know people who experience this yearning, but the burden of their money makes real change difficult. They might even live modest lives (we can learn a great deal from the wealthy about saving money), but what do they finally gain? Like many of us, they share the sense of not having enough. They push their money first in one direction and then in another, from one cause to the next, but none of it brings happiness.

We need to understand that defining ourselves by external measures invariably leads to the pressures associated with such concerns. Yet even in the midst of stress, the yearning for simplicity still exists, even if we aren't aware of it. We can only overcome the pressures brought on by external circumstances when we ground ourselves in a different life.

In the opening chapter of his Confessions, *St. Augustine says, "You have made us for Yourself, O Lord, and our hearts know no rest until they rest in You," expressing the sense of how useless it is to experience spiritual yearning if we continue to give ourselves over to external things. As the Spanish mystic Teresa of Avila says simply in one of her poems, "God alone is enough."*

What a provocative idea. Isn't this truth born out in our own experience? I've recently bought a new car but soon discover I want a newer, larger model. Only weeks into a new job, I'm already looking for another way to advance my career. Shortly after winning the affection of the woman I've been seeing, I'm searching for my next conquest. Each of these situations expresses the unrelenting force of our desires.

I find it a marvelous experience to put on my monastic habit; in this simple act of preparation I feel appropriately clothed. In contrast, when I am preparing to go out for an appointment unrelated to my professional life and work as a monk, I find myself searching through the clothes in my closet for the right thing to wear. No one is there to give me advice or choose my clothes for me. I often find that this or that article of clothing needs ironing or mending, and these tasks loom larger than they actually are. For monks, the question of clothing is settled in a very practical way by our habit, allowing us freedom from the question of how to attire ourselves. This small matter offers great relief! I'm not concerned with designer clothing and don't need to consider which outfit to wear for a trip or when I'm invited out. In such situations we often find ourselves making decisions based on what another person expects—or what we think they expect. We may even feel captive to the demands of others.

While it is a challenge to free ourselves from the expectations of those who have formed a particular image of us, growing into adulthood means working to free ourselves from being pressured by what other people think.

Let's consider the matter of status symbols. When you find yourself at a social event or reception, reflect on how much energy people waste worrying about dressing according to the rules they feel they need follow. Or consider our fascination with professional titles. Many people are quite happy to bestow titles on others because this allows them to say, "I have just spoken with an extraordinary person!"

We sometimes think spending time with an important person will increase our own worth, as if we could decorate ourselves with their aura. The chance to have a private audience with the pope, for example, gives many people a great sense of elevation, and many would pay large amounts of money to have such an experience. But only the present is incorruptible.

I find such an attitude questionable, especially if the primary intention is to take a photograph—as it often seems to be with the pope. But if someone says, "I admire this person because of his spirituality, the way he lives his life, and I want to meet him because I believe that he might open something within me and further my own spiritual life," this doesn't bother me at all.

How we accommodate the expectations of others is often shaped by the experience we have with our own parents. As we move through life, our partner, our children, or our neighbor occupy that role. In order to break this pattern and become a more complete person, we need a point of orientation. Faith gives us the best one we could possibly find.

In terms of meeting the expectations of others, many seem to know exactly what an Abbot Primate like myself should, and should not, do. Particularly, they are concerned that he should not deign to lower himself in such and such a way. When I consider what others would prohibit me from doing, I am confounded—sometimes to the point of anger. These expectations prompt me to find special delight in giving concerts with my rock band. The diverse responses I experience are fascinating: some people accept it but look sideways at me; others genuinely think it's great because it validates their own unique desires and suggests that surface appearances don't need to determine the way they live their lives.

Consider the style of clothing that prevails among employees at a given company. Is someone a better comptroller or marketing agent simply because he or she wears a particular suit? Certainly not. I delight in individuals who do not flout the status quo on principle but rather have the courage to express their individuality. Unfortunately, most genuine individuals in our society are continually pressed to defend or explain themselves.

Certain occasions, such as attending a formal celebration, call for appropriate clothing to honor the event. But even these occasions necessitate limits. If a woman feels the need to spend five hours at the salon to make certain her hair is perfect, something is amiss.

Less Is More

Reducing can be both important and helpful. As earlier suggested, fasting as a spiritual discipline is a good expression of this practice. The biblical practices of almsgiving (offering assistance to those in need) and prayer also contribute to the idea of less is more.

However, many choose to fast in order to enhance their beauty or better their health, nullifying the spiritual dimension altogether. It's certainly not a bad thing to eat less in order to lose weight, but this kind of discipline has nothing to do with fasting for religious reasons.

Jesus also reminds us that it does not please God when we fast in order to be seen by others (see Matt. 6:16–18). Benedict speaks to this matter in his Rule, suggesting that an abbot should not impose particularly arduous demands on the brothers: "Let each one deny himself some food, drink, sleep, needless talking and idle jesting" (RB 49.7). A monk should submit all his plans to the abbot; otherwise he runs the risk of becoming proud of his spirituality—entirely missing the goal of the Christian life.

Religious fasting can make us alert to the true nature of our lives. Someone once told me about a weekend he spent with a friend on retreat at a monastery. His friend's arrival was delayed, and the man had to take his dinner alone. There was nothing in his room to distract him—no newspaper, no television, no friend. Only a cheese sandwich and a cup of peppermint tea. When his friend finally arrived, the man greeted him by saying, "You know what? I've not had such a delicious cheese sandwich for a long time, and the tea was superb. It was like an explosion of taste!"

How do we explain this experience? For once, the man wasn't distracted by other things. This dimension of fasting can be practiced at any time, not only during seasons traditionally set aside for this purpose, like Lent. This is not about the mortification of the flesh—to recall a traditional intention—or denial of our desires; rather, it has to do with awakening our awareness. Fasting can help us rediscover gratitude.

I take great joy in something as simple as sipping a cup of cool water or eating a piece of dark bread. When I chew food slowly and consciously, I find myself able to taste it so much more fully!

In the Gospels' approach to this question, another factor comes to the fore. The portion we are encouraged to give up in terms of consumption is what we ought to give to the poor. Fasting therefore becomes a matter of sharing with others, transforming the invitation to deny ourselves into a denial for the sake of others. In the process, we attain greater freedom, and others are able to benefit from our sacrifice. We find ourselves renewed according to the communitarian impulses found in the Bible.

This leads us to the third spiritual practice found in the Scriptures: almsgiving, which is given the same importance as prayer and fasting (see Matt. 6). Giving to others in need expresses our trust that God will give us all that we need. Whether we have only a little or great wealth, we are to consider what it is that we are able to give.

In the sixth chapter of Matthew's Gospel, Jesus reminds us that the left hand should not know what the right hand is doing. At stake here is our liberation from pride and vanity. Perhaps you know of charitable organizations that do much good in the world. But what often seems to matter in such charitable acts is that others notice the gift. We've all sat on park benches marked with a plaque that declares who donated them.

In the United States, organizations commonly publish brochures announcing which persons or groups have given money. Such gifts are categorized—a kind of publicity that recognizes the donors and how much they gave. In contrast to Germany and many European countries, citizens in the United States pay far lower taxes to cover universal social services; it is generally expected that the wealthy will give voluntarily to organizations like parish schools and hospitals. Such gifts are presumed to be a moral obligation.

When I give to the needy, I find myself beginning to serve others, which is a fundamental Christian attitude: to serve rather than to rule.

In the time of Jesus, insurance and retirement plans did not exist, but the poor certainly did—widows, orphans, and strangers who did not belong to Jewish society. These are the people God is particularly concerned about. In Psalm 146, we read:

Happy are those whose help is the God of Jacob,
    whose hope is in the Lord *their God,*
who made heaven and earth,
    the sea, and all that is in them;
who keeps faith forever,
    who executes justice for the oppressed;
    who gives food to the hungry.

The Lord *sets the prisoners free;*
    the Lord *opens the eyes of the blind.*
The Lord *lifts up those who are bowed down;*
    the Lord *loves the righteous.*

> The LORD *watches over strangers;*
> *he upholds the orphan and the widow. (Psalm 146:5–9)*

This passage focuses on the oppressed—the hungry, the prisoners, the blind, the bowed down, the ones who are treated unjustly—and also strangers, orphans, and widows. Jesus mentions these same people in Matthew's Gospel: "Just as you did it to one of the least of these who are members of my family, you did it to me" (see Matt. 25:31–46).

What part does God play in the fate of the very poor? Why doesn't God take care of such people? God is present to them through the work that we do. God did not make the world for only a few people, but for all of us.

Such texts have a burning and even explosive power in our lives, reminding us that the world exists for everyone. God also knows that we are not all mindful or fortunate enough to be able to participate fully, which is one justification for the social welfare systems in our economies. Attending to the market economy is not sufficient; we must also consider how to address the social welfare of all members of society and seek a proper balance that is just for all.

Serving Rather than Ruling

Encountering the Holy Scriptures can be quite uncomfortable, particularly when we have become so comfortable in our lives! To ascertain what we should and can do for others is not always a simple matter. We must dig deep and engage ourselves intensely. God has not promised to give us comfort; and in many situations it would befit us to be much more active than we are. Alfred Herrhausen, for example, worked toward a forgiveness of debts among developing nations in an attempt to establish a more just balance in the world. He pointed out that many nations had already paid back the principal on their loans. The debt to be forgiven was the interest on those loans. Doing so would free these nations of their heavy burden so that they could better develop their economies.

This sort of economic forgiveness exemplifies the idea of "serving rather than ruling" and can be applied in much smaller ways. Mother Teresa's remarkable work among the poor of Calcutta reminds us that we might not be able to heal those who are sick and dying, but we can surely be a presence of mercy and compassion for them in their need.

We shouldn't allow ourselves to hide behind her example by thinking, *Yes—but she's Mother Teresa.* When we spend time with a sick neighbor or comfort friends when a loved one dies by simply being present, we serve them. Those who are able to "weep with those who weep" (Rom. 12:15) or offer nourishing food are important.

In times of suffering, we do not always know what to say. It is often enough simply to be present with those who are sad and need consolation. Each of us can do this where we live. When we open our eyes to the needs around us, we begin to see much that we can do.

In the political sphere, we often have the impression that things are relatively fine, but when I think of the poverty crisis among children I know this is not so. I recently read the biography of the evangelical Bernd Siggelkow, who in 1995 founded the Arche community in Berlin, an organization committed to helping children and young people. This organization does not receive a penny of support from the government and in recent years has expanded to eight centers, which together offer more than a thousand children living under the poverty line meals as well as love and support. And this is in Germany! These children have great physical needs, but their emotional needs are even greater; many of them have been abandoned. As our society turns more people away, the help we can offer matters even more.

Behind the maxim "serving rather than ruling" is a simple premise concerning the way we choose to live our lives. Do we want power and its corresponding appearance of status, or do we want to serve others? Another nuance of this idea involves using our strength to take a powerful stance for the wellbeing of others before ourselves.

Caring is a part of serving—an act of accompanying and attending to the needs of others in order to offer encouragement. In doing so, we extend to them a new and liberating perspective by which to live their lives.

To Live Differently Is Possible

Of course we can choose to live differently. Recently, I had lunch with a young African man who has quite a different experience of reducing than my own. Benedictines have an international commission on Benedictine education that meets every three years, gathering several hundred teachers from many nations of the world. We come together to explore the question, "What shapes the character of education in our Benedictine schools?" On the student level, some three hundred young people gather for the same kind of conversation. We've recently coordinated this event with the World Youth Congresses in order to make it more financially sustainable. I consider these gatherings a matter of the highest importance because they allow German teachers to better understand the educational situation in African schools and in the life experiences of Africans. Books alone cannot teach us what we need to know; the insights and lessons we learn directly from others are essential.

To believe and live a Christian life does not mean to remain in the shelter of the familiar. Lift up your head and look around to see what life looks like for others.

An acquaintance of mine recounted for me his experience of an "angel week" spent at the sea. He stood every day—all day—in the water, and each evening ate a simple meal prepared over an open fire. "We sat together on the beach as the sun went down, by the crackling fire, eating half-cooked and sooty potatoes—and knew that we were the happiest people in the world!" His life was shaped by the freedom he experienced spending the day in nature with others and enjoying the sustenance of an undercooked potato.

Learning to limit our lives through sacrifice can be a great good if we let go of the things we don't really need.

Think for a moment of all the things you pay for: a large house, a car, a flat-screen television. Such things can exert substantial pressure on our lives. I am certain that the easiest way to make people unhappy is to give them a lot of money.

What would it be like for us to live without our money and things? What if we took one step backwards and found ourselves surrounded by people who liked us because of who we are and not because of what we own? How important is it for us to be friends with people who find the idea of simplicity ridiculous, perhaps because it calls into question their own lives? Do I really want to be esteemed by them?

With God, our backup is always secure.

I'd like to read and hear more about authentic and alternative paths that others have found in their lives. Instead of the negative stories we so often encounter, I'd like to know more about people whose lives offer real encouragement. Learning about those who care for others in need can embolden us. Is it really true that we don't want to have our lives called into question? While we need to know about situations of abuse and tragedy, we ought to develop compassion in order to encourage our own potential and give ourselves to what is positive.

Periods of solitude can help us develop such a capacity, enabling us to let go and reduce our consumption. If we devote our energies to cultivating this way of being, we'll find ourselves freed of many burdens. Not only will we be able to move through life with a greater sense of fulfillment, but we will also establish the general framework needed to experience the richness of Christian faith described in the first section of this book.

In this second section, we've explored the question of what we can do in order to know God more deeply, allowing him more effectively into our lives. In the third section, we turn aside from the question of what we are to do and devote ourselves to better understanding the interior posture that makes an authentic and living relationship with God possible.

life with God

Saying Yes Within

What can I make of my life when I live it with God? This question points to a revolutionary perspective. Faith offers an entirely different approach, one freed from the illusions of success and happiness so dominant in our day.

A famous story is told about the desert monastic father St. Anthony. When he was about twenty years old, he found himself seized by the passage from the Gospels, "If you want to be happy, then go, sell what you have and give it to the poor." Anthony took this call seriously. After he made sure that his sister was cared for, he followed Jesus's command and gave away the rest of his wealth to the poor. He then retreated to the desert. Through this act Anthony changed his life completely, committing himself to a radical way.

A similar event took place in the life of Ignatius Loyola. This remarkable man, who came from a noble family and would later go on to found the Society of Jesus, was wounded in battle and subsequently found himself brought to the monastery in Montserrat. After making his confession, he laid his weapons on the altar and retreated to pursue a life of solitude. In the same way, Benedict (the father of our order) turned from his studies and career at the age of twenty and retreated to live in a cave in the cliffs above Subiaco.

These are remarkable sorts of men who probably never imagined that a life of faith could be dull.

When we take faith seriously, it can challenge and expand the sense we have of our potential. We must risk approaching faith in a radical way, rooting ourselves in its fundamental truths. Only then can we discover how faith might become the foundation for our lives.

In Matthew's Gospel, Jesus speaks to this way when he says, "If you wish to be perfect, go, sell your possessions, and give the money to the poor, and you will have treasure in heaven; then come, follow me" (Matt. 19:21). This radical call comes in the form of a principled life decision.

Determination is the true witness of our spiritual forbears. Many might find such a radicality discouraging, suggesting that people like Benedict lived in different times when such decisions were easier to make. I am not suggesting that everyone should sell all they have and enter a monastery. The transmission of such stories into our context might mean giving ourselves to others to the extent that everything else pales in significance. Such a shift inevitably turns us away from the pursuit of our own interests.

A beautiful image that clarifies my point is marriage, which in some respects can be compared to this decision of faith. Two people become acquainted and fall in love, learning to trust each other in a deepening way. Many married people have shared with me that marriage eventually leads them to say yes to their partner first, and vice versa.

Faith is much like the way that we give ourselves radically to another person in marriage in order to experience the true depth of relationship possible between a man and a woman. We make a decision to live our lives with God, in good times and bad; we don't throw up our hands in despair when things don't go as well as we'd hoped. As in a marriage, we will certainly experience high and low points, periods of strong presence and times when we feel as if we're wandering alone. In times of need, faith stands firm as a source of help, offering a positive perspective within which to live our lives.

The decisions we make every day are the occasions that give shape to our lives. One example is our choice of a profession, which sometimes leads to our calling. I know teachers who approach their job as a genuine service to young people. There are also judges, lawyers, and politicians who conduct themselves on the basis of their Christian convictions with a strong sense of responsibility. Such people are far more common than we sometimes imagine, though we are not publicly aware of their commitment.

We can also make a decision to devote ourselves to what brings strength and to turn away from what discourages. I know a group of politicians who gather each year in January for a week's retreat in a monastery. Their decision leads them out of the "faster, higher, farther" mentality that dominates so much of our daily life—an unnatural rhythm characterized by too much work and too little sleep. Retreat can help us recover the concentration we need for our work. In this case, it might even lead to a healthier kind of political discourse, precisely because these men have taken time to root themselves anew in the deep wellsprings of their lives.

In the midst of daily life, these are positive examples for those attempting to find strength and the proper coordinates for a faithful orientation. Every one of us can begin where we are; slowly but surely we can live a life rooted in the depths of God.

I was once invited to accompany this particular group of politicians for one weekend of their annual retreat. On Sunday I told them: "We will conclude our time together after this morning's Eucharist, and you'll go home to your families. This is crucial, since you'll find yourselves accomplishing your work much more effectively when you remain connected to the things that bring you strength." Many people ignore such advice, working twelve or fourteen hour days and living always beyond their limits without taking time for themselves or their loved ones.

A Gentle Revolution

To step outside of the pressure that demands achievement can change the world. Jesus once claimed that those who see themselves as important always seek out the places of greatest honor. We see this truth eloquently illustrated in the story of Zebedee's sons. Their mother wanted to secure places for them at Jesus's right hand and left—a request that brought a sharp rebuke (see Matt. 20:20–23).

Jesus had just spoken of the suffering he would face, yet his disciples had nothing better to do than quarrel with each other about who among them was better or more important. Jesus interrupted them with these words: "You know that the rulers of the Gentiles lord it over them, and their great ones are tyrants over them. It will not be so among you; but whoever wishes to be great among you must be your servant, and whoever wishes to be first among you must be your slave; just as the Son of Man came not to be served but to serve, and to give his life a ransom for many" (Matt. 20:25–28).

If investment bankers and leaders in both the financial sector and industry would take the call to serve others seriously, we might experience something of a Copernican Revolution in our society—one that turned from the incessant focus on personal gain toward a concern for others' wellbeing. After all, such people are responsible not only for the small circle in which they live their personal lives, but also for many people of this earth. Considering the nature of the globalized world we inhabit, their actions and decisions have consequences for the welfare of many. They must be aware of the fact that a portion of the world's population becomes increasingly richer while another part sinks deeper into poverty.

This is not simply a matter of fate, nor is it the fault of those who are at the bottom of the proverbial pyramid; their actions also have a significant impact in this scenario. To maintain that the life of the poor is improved by earning more money, thus contributing higher tax support for the wellbeing of the whole, misses the point altogether. The selfishness of such financiers has, in effect, plunged many families into terrible need.

Responsibility for Creation

A different and more humble approach to life conveys a clear yes to creation. However, many people in our society subjugate nature to the point that they no longer have a proper sense of measure. They exploit it at any cost, as if nature has been given to them to do as they please. Nature is not simply at our disposal. Acting as though it is casts us in the role of the sorcerer's apprentice; at a certain point we no longer have power over the consequences of our actions.

Perhaps we are becoming more circumspect in such matters. The dramatic catastrophe of the BP oil spill in the Gulf of Mexico was a wakeup call for many people. We witnessed millions of tons of oil spewing into the gulf, but where is our shock now? We seem to have already lost this sense of proportionality—the proper measure of our actions and attitudes. A yes to creation ought to awaken within us a sense of humility. Serving nature and serving other human beings should go hand in hand.

Rather than merely taking notice, we must allow ourselves to be stirred to action by these experiences. So often we react in horror to images of a catastrophe on the news but five minutes later turn our thoughts to other matters entirely.

We need to cultivate a broad horizon of perspective and responsibility. Allow me to offer other examples in which cultivating such a point of view is important.

Christianity is the most practiced religion in the world, yet in many nations Christians are pushed to the margins of society. So what do we do? Sit comfortably in front of our screens watching the news and eating our chips.

In the summer of 2010, something happened that struck me as a matter of importance. Colonel Muammar Gaddafi visited Rome and arranged for a staff of three hundred to attend to his needs. He gave each person a copy of the Qur'an and promised rewards to any who became Muslim. Three apparently did. Since Gaddafi found nothing wrong in advocating for his faith, it seems he should have allowed Christians in his country to do the same. Yet if I traveled to Libya, I could not even carry a Bible. This kind of disparity is genuinely dangerous.

Let's turn to another issue. To my mind, the declining birthrate in Germany is a genuine tragedy for our society. Families are obviously responsible for this decline, but it may also be caused by insufficient public attention to the joy that children bring. The false notion that a child stands in the way of a woman's professional development and opportunities is prevalent. Other countries deal with this issue in better ways, including greater financial incentives and childcare for families with children. Children are not the product of money but of love. We should make a fundamental decision and say yes to a way of life that makes room for children, even when it requires sacrifice. In every case this experience brings more joy and satisfaction than we can imagine, even as it preserves creation.

We need commentators who address these social problems, but the pressure of being politically correct too often silences the expression of our convictions. To put it another way: we are considering which insurance plan to take out on our house as it burns down around us.

Overcoming Fear

What lies behind our behavior is often fear.

Faith in God, given the plethora of psychological entanglements we face, can be a healing force. When we understand that we're never alone, that we don't have to do everything on our own, and that we're allowed to make mistakes, we find our burden lightened to the point of being able to overcome our neurotic fears.

This faith has the power to change our lives here and now—and not only in cases of suffering and death. No one lives forever; sooner or later we must each face mortality. When we do, we can be encouraged by our belief in the Resurrection and can approach God into eternal happiness rather than as an abstraction concerned with the hereafter.

When we succeed in finding our way to joy, we will discover ourselves healed of much that troubles us. Faith relieves us of the great burden of fear we often carry. This discovery presumes that we have not been given the image of a condemning God.

In the same way that faith can give people suffering from serious illnesses a perspective by which to face their challenges, it can also take away the fear that often causes us to give up. Faith can bestow a sense of humility that discourages us from exploiting nature and the people within it. Faith can effect courage, love, and creativity; it has the power to support a couple in their decision to sacrifice income and career in order to bring a child into the world.

However, many people in our society have been given a dreadful image of God. Nothing could be further from the truth than a God who lays in wait to expose our failings in order to condemn us. As the apostle John writes in his First Letter: "There is no fear in love, but perfect love casts out fear; for fear has to do with punishment, and whoever fears has not reached perfection in love" (1 Jn. 4:18).

To provoke fear in others toward God—who only wants us to live in freedom—is a deplorable act.

"Be not afraid!" we hear repeatedly throughout the Bible. We might inscribe these words on a banner over us when we make a decision to live by faith in all things and not only in difficult times. What a powerful maxim: "Be not afraid!"

Once as I descended in an elevator, I found myself face to face with a young woman dressed in punk who, seeing me, screamed aloud. Remembering the words of Jesus I said to her, grinning, "Don't be afraid; it is I!" She laughed! I doubt if she knew these were words taken from the Bible. Marvelous! So often when we find ourselves falling into some panic or another, God must come to us and say, "Don't be afraid; it is I!"

Isn't the prospect of a life without fear wonderful? Even if we make great mistakes, God is always with us. In faith we find a perspective that opens us to the future!

Living Without Worries

Faith is not merely an intellectual form of knowing. Faith is a form of trust in the future, a future of *God-with-us*. In faith, we find ourselves able to risk the future with great trust. Those familiar with the Scriptures might recognize the Exodus of the

Israelites as a foundational image describing our way with God—or, more accurately, God's way with us. The path wasn't easy, but it finally led God's people to the Promised Land.

In the face of such a claim, many questions and doubts remain, but it never helps to worry about something before it happens. A marvelous passage in Luke's Gospel encourages us to face whatever might come:

Consider the ravens: they neither sow nor reap, they have neither storehouse nor barn, and yet God feeds them. Of how much more value are you than the birds! And can any of you by worrying add a single hour to your span of life? If then you are not able to do so small a thing as that, why do you worry about the rest? Consider the lilies, how they grow: they neither toil nor spin; yet I tell you, even Solomon in all his glory was not clothed like one of these. But if God so clothes the grass of the field, which is alive today and tomorrow is thrown into the oven, how much more will he clothe you—you of little faith! And do not keep striving for what you are to eat and what you are to drink, and do not keep worrying. For it is the nations of the world that strive after all these things, and your Father knows that you need them. Instead, strive for his kingdom, and these things will be given to you as well. (Lk. 12:24–31)

This does not mean that we should cease from our labors and presume to let ourselves be carried along in our lives. Rather, we should be and act according to our nature. Without diminishing the worries that can otherwise crush us, we should take responsibility for our lives.

We seem to have dispensed with living in the present moment. As a result we exaggerate our thoughts and concerns for the future. The art of living in the present—reading and reflecting and praying in the now—is vital. Tomorrow is tomorrow. To live in this manner is a great art!

During my many visits to Africa, I've been struck by how Africans experience the present in a natural manner. They find delight in the experience of something good. In a powerful way, they understand that sooner or later they'll have nothing—or quite a bit less than they do now. In the moment they don't dwell on this reality because they know that life is happening now.

Can we decide to shape our lives by committing to live with this kind of awareness? Doesn't such an attitude finally hit against the hard edges of reality, such as when someone becomes unemployed and must face the myriad challenges that arise as a result?

Facing such an experience is indeed difficult; at times we must simply accept what life brings. In such circumstances we find ourselves carried by a simple trust that God stands with us and will help us find a way through. A beautiful saying comes to mind: "When God closes a door, he opens a window!" As long as we stare at the closed door and insist on passing through it, we might never notice the open window behind us.

Perhaps you've experienced a situation in which your soul was illumined with a great brightness, if only for a moment. Perhaps you recall a particular yearning that came over you on a walk or at a burial service. Suddenly, you found some part of your soul, which otherwise was dark with shadows, bathed in light. Take courage and focus the spotlight of your attention on this experience. A funeral can provide a good opportunity to experience a real illumination of the heart. We must learn to trust, to look behind our fears. The knowledge that God is with us in our journey can alleviate the weight of our burdens. We don't have to overachieve, and we needn't do everything ourselves.

Opening Ourselves

I often find that when I bring a request to God a solution seems to hang in the air before me until someone simply asks: "Do you have a few minutes? I'd like to speak with you." Something quite different usually comes forth than what I expected.

It could well be that God has planned another path for us than the one we imagine. This realization demands and establishes a certain kind of flexibility; everything doesn't need occur as we envision it. When we are convinced that God loves us, we find ourselves capable of approaching life with a trusting attitude, even in difficult situations.

I know someone who tells me that it's a good thing, and a significant step, to allow God to show me his way. The questions that arise in the midst of critical circumstances in our lives often indicate the reflexive nature of our response: "How can God let something like that happen?" To pose the question in this way is a mistake; it demonstrates that we don't yet understand the God we encounter on the cross.

When facing difficult situations, almost everyone asks, "Why me? What did I do wrong?"

But is it always the case that someone is wrong in such circumstances? Couldn't we just as easily say, "I'm ready to take the good with the bad. Through this experience I can learn more about who God is"?

If God were required to make judgments on the basis of my interpretation of the good, he would quickly find himself cornered. God does not promise to protect us from difficulty. His message is entirely different: "I am always with you, and I will care for you even in the difficult circumstances you will face."

For this reason, we can trust that not a single experience is without meaning. The apostle Paul writes, "We know that all things work together for good for those who love God" (Rom. 8:28). This verse suggests that I must undergo my own deep experiences and allow my life to be changed by them.

In retrospect, many of us who have undergone difficult periods in life often comment upon how much we learned. For example, accepting a serious illness and coming to terms with one's mortality can be a powerful learning experience.

In my last visit to the annual meeting of the Benedictine superiors in South Africa, the speaker was an Anglican monk with prosthetic hands and an artificial eye. He had been active in the struggle for freedom and democracy in Zimbabwe. As a result of his work, he received a letter bomb from an opponent to the movement. The explosion left him seriously wounded. During his hospitalization and recovery, he underwent a profound spiritual transformation and now travels the world speaking about the need to overcome violence. As an authentic spokesman for this cause, he finds his efforts on behalf of peace are more effective and reach a much wider audience. Tragedy introduced him to a new mission.

Let me offer another example. Recently someone told me about a lecture given by a man who had just turned sixty and was suffering from multiple sclerosis. He stood straight as an arrow and was dynamic, full of life, and a deep believer. In the course of his remarks, he acknowledged his struggle with anger and doubt, but at a certain point he told himself: "You're asking the wrong question! The question should not be, 'Why am I sick at this point in my life—why *me?*' I realized that I'd been striding through my life for almost sixty years in full health. Perhaps I should have been wondering, '*Why* is this happening to me?'" In the course of his life he had rarely paused from his work to sit and listen. He recognized that his disease might offer him the chance to live with greater awareness and intention.

"Why?" is often the wrong question. "Where to now?" takes us much farther.

A changed vantage point can promote healing when we find ourselves facing difficulties. I often observe this in situations where one of the partners in a long marriage dies. Such a loss is painful and may even feel catastrophic to the widow or widower; many who face this situation remain overcome with anguish. But it's possible to realize that every experience of happiness comes to an end sooner or later. Instead of getting trapped in our grief, we might say, "I am grateful that I was able to spend so many years with my partner, sharing so much that was beautiful together."

Hanging onto circumstances in our lives as if they will never change or end is a form of self-inflicted pain. We must eventually face the deep and primal fear that governs such a clinging posture. I believe that the experience of coming to terms with our own mortality frees us to live more consciously and with deeper intention, though it can be a challenge to maneuver our way through such emotional impasses.

A young man once shared with me a powerful experience he had while attending a particular funeral. Advanced in age, the widow of the deceased came attired in a white dress as if she was attending her own wedding. Nothing in her manner seemed contrived or affected. During the service, the family recognized how deeply sad she was, but the woman did not want to deny the other dimension of her experience: her joy in knowing that her husband—the father of her children, a man who had suffered many years from cancer—was now released from his pain and in death had found his way into the glory of God. At the end of the service, the people who had gathered were not offered a piece of stale cake but were invited to partake of a sumptuous meal, a feast appropriate to a celebration.

This view of death can liberate our experience of mourning. For many people, death is only an ending, an enduring loss. For Christians, the matter is quite different: we believe that the best is reserved for us after death. While we should certainly honor the sorrow experienced by those who lose a dear friend, our entrance into heaven entitles us to a bit of joy, however trite that might sound.

An old abbot I once knew put it this way: "We live our lives toward eternity, but the journey in the meantime is wonderful. Eternity can gladly wait a little bit."

Learning to Listen with Our Heart

"Listen carefully, my son, to the master's instructions, and attend to them with the ear of your heart. This is advice from a father who loves you; welcome it, and faithfully put it into practice." These words stand at the very beginning of the Prologue to Benedict's Rule. A conscious posture of listening suggests an openness of heart for what God holds. Those who live in an intimate relationship with God discover much that is beautiful, things that others miss because their focus is negative.

The discoveries that follow from this sort of listening are not necessarily spectacular. It's often much more important to recognize little things and pass them on to others. For example, when a child comes home with a poor report card we might say in a quiet tone of voice: "Next time it will surely be better. We'll work on it together! The most important thing is not the grade, after all, but the fact that we have each other!" Paying attention to children and encouraging them can be much more consequential than the most significant achievements made in global politics.

Too often, we don't allow God to reveal exactly what kind of person he is. The same is true in human relationships. Many marriages fall apart because one partner expects the other to live up to certain expectations, and this is a recipe for failure. All those who are married must overcome this stumbling block. A marriage only becomes deeply satisfying when we come to recognize that the other is an individual person in his or her own right, complete with quirks and limitations. We are the same. Can we allow each other to be as we are and still experience love in the midst of acceptance?

In the monastery, I sometimes encounter a brother who is difficult to get along with. This irritation remains until I engage him with greater intentionality, attempting to approach him from various sides of his personality in order to better recognize who he really is. In the process, I encounter his idealism and am reminded of the fact that he, too, has taken permanent vows to the life we share. He is as loved by God as I am. Realizing this truth dispenses with much that is otherwise difficult about him, and I find myself beginning to discover him as a true gift.

We call this practice "mindfulness"; it is the call to live by means of a mindful attitude. Try addressing God with this petition: "Lead me more mindfully in my life so that I might perceive others in a different way. Help me consider my environment, my fellow human beings, and my work." Prayer animates our attempts to lead a more mindful life.

We must learn to be more gracious to ourselves and to others. God prepares and enables us by always being ready to forgive.

Discovering Mercy Anew

If there were not a merciful God, I could not go on living as I do. I believe that if we are honest with ourselves, we will recognize the guilt we carry for our actions. It is marvelous to realize that God forgives us for everything—even when we feel we don't deserve it. As Benedict instructs his fellow monks: "Never lose hope in God's mercy" (*Rule*, Ch. 4.74).

Mercy may seem old-fashioned, but its value is beyond compare! The idea that monks treat each other with mercy can bring tears to the eyes of many whose reality, whether at work or in marriage, bears little or no resemblance.

"Be merciful, just as your Father is merciful," the Scriptures remind us (Lk. 6:36). This verse encapsulates what life could be if we had the courage to live from the depth of our Christian faith.

An eloquent parallel can be found in First Peter: "Be holy, because I am holy" (1 Pet. 1:16 NIV; see also Lev. 19:2). Apparently, holiness stands in relation to mercy. "Judge not, that you be not judged" (Matt. 7:1 NKJV) is another clear indication of the relationship between holiness and mercy, or to recall the passage cited by the founder of our order: "He will not break a bruised reed" (Matt. 12:20). To strengthen the weak, to help the needy, and to be simply present for others: these are experiences that cannot be measured in terms of monetary value.

When two people argue, they take on a debt toward each other. The quarrel disturbs them both because they are sitting in the same boat. Ultimately, both are guilty and in need of forgiveness, an awareness that becomes clear when one of them forgives the other. As Jesus taught us to pray, "Forgive us our debts, as we also have forgiven our debtors" (Matt. 6:12).

God's forgiveness is abundant as we hear described in the parable of the prodigal son, which in German we call "the lost son." This story offers such rich insights into our faith! A young person can hardly expect to understand it completely. Only later in life can we begin to grasp the liberating power of forgiveness. That said, our recognition of mercy does not lead us to approach life in a nonchalant manner so that we become indifferent to what we do or leave undone; rather, it is an awareness that awakens us to the inevitability of failure and guilt.

God's light is so great that I can create no shadows in his sight. This light covers every sin and every shadow our lives cast. When our own guilt or that of another grips us, we remain stuck in the past. This is a vicious circle—what we call a "devil's circle"—that can only be broken by receiving God's forgiveness and sharing it with others, thereby relinquishing our guilt in order to entrust it to God.

The fact that God forgives us ought to be the primary message we experience when we make our confession. When my monastic brothers come to sit in the confessional, I always tell them, "Be merciful; encouragement is not as important as absolution!"— which is to say, we all need to experience what it means to be forgiven. The saying of Jesus also holds true: "Go, and sin no more!" (John 8:11 NJKV). Confession and forgiveness are not an easy matter, but the process is an honest one. It calls us to admit that we have sinned so that we can experience God's forgiveness. This is a remarkable truth and a liberating realization.

Living Without Fear of Touch

In the presence of God, we must hide nothing. No sin holds him back from the desire to turn toward us.

"I am the way, the truth, and the life," Jesus says. When we consider his example we discover the fascinating truth that he always turned toward sinners. We particularly need him in the areas of our lives riddled with guilt.

Jesus sought out and healed those who were unloved, prone to failure, and despised by others in society. We speak of a God who goes deliberately to the place that hurts. To borrow an image from soccer, it's something like a good forward directly in front of the goal. We are not talking about a fair weather God, but rather one who confronted the Pharisees and delighted in eating with tax collectors and sinners. In eastern cultures such as Jesus's, eating together means far more than it does in our society. Table fellowship is a way to demonstrate that we are one with those with whom we eat.

In the same way we are able to help others who have fallen in need. Serving means being with the other, offering them our company, and attending to them so that we can experience their need firsthand.

When we open ourselves to God and take to heart what he says to us—even if it is surprising or entirely different from what we expected—we find that our sight is altered. As we live into this experience, we find ourselves developing a deepening understanding about how we might view our lives from God's perspective. In this way, our heart widens, and we find that we are able to face whatever comes to us with greater trust.

This altered perspective leads us away from the question "Why?" and encourages us to ask "Where now?" instead. When we learn to tune in to the quiet frequency of God, our relationships and ourselves begin to change. Mercy and forgiveness become a part of our lives, and suddenly things no longer seem quite so impossible. This is what it means to grow in faith!

Letting Another Guide Us

How does God speak to us today? How can we allow ourselves to be addressed and led by God?

My own call to monastic life happened as a fourteen-year-old. I had wanted to become a teacher and raise a family until a pamphlet I found in the attic of our house opened my life in a new way. When I read the story of missionaries to the islands of the South Seas, I had the sense that Jesus Christ needed *me*, that this would be *my* life's path. It was as if a door opened. When I reflect on this, it is clear that God revealed possibilities to me that I might not otherwise have sought or decided of my own volition.

Many people today give themselves entirely to God in terms of their life's journey. Of course I can sustain my own ideas, but I should stay open to the greater reality of God in my life. When he places something in my heart, I ought to consider it very carefully.

I never sat down to develop a strategy but have simply allowed people and situations to come my way, together with the inevitable challenges life brings. When I was elected Abbot Primate of our monastic order, I accepted the office because I became convinced that my vocation required it of me. At that time our order was approached by Zen Buddhist leaders, and I gladly welcomed their inquiries. As a result, we developed a structured conversation that became known as Monastic Interreligious Dialogue (MID, www.monasticdialog.com). Later, we initiated new building projects in China for the expansion of our order in Asia. China had long been drawing my interest, but I never imagined it possible to move ahead in this sphere; we eventually built a large hospital there. The idea of being responsible for all of the contractual negotiations involved in the planning of this hospital was beyond my comprehension, but I was able to do it with God's help. Many other unanticipated projects have enriched my life since I entered this office.

Conversation with God has been and remains important for me in the midst of all these tasks. Many people seem overwhelmed by the plans they undertake—for themselves, their company, their children, or their vacation. Where will we be in five years? What do I need today? In our struggle to manage time, these stresses often leave us feeling greatly overwhelmed and burdened.

People often ask me the same question: "How will it be for you in five years?" I don't know and can't know. Frankly, the question doesn't interest me. I have enough to address in the tasks that are immediately before me.

For example, our plan to found monastic communities in places where our order isn't active has brought both resistance and support. Our first endeavor was in the Philippines; in our next venture I found myself helping establish European monasteries in Africa. These plans came to me as matters of necessity; it was no more complicated than that. I listened and tried to bring into being what I heard. God revealed his presence throughout these initiatives, with astonishing developments along the way.

After the break-up of colonialism, two of our four abbeys in Tanzania were populated only with European monks, a situation that made us realize there were no longer sufficient brothers in our European monasteries. These mission outposts were made into parishes and attached to dioceses. What does our new order look like? We've set much in motion and must be careful things don't come to a standstill. Africans themselves should grow into leadership in the same way that a shoemaker's apprentice learns both the skills of the trade and how to run a business.

As recently as two years ago, I was glad to see that two-thirds of the brothers in these communities are Africans. Things are going well, and several African monks have taken on leadership offices. Of course, there are disappointments—some monks have already left—but this is no different from what we experience in the European context.

Maturing in Faith

What does all this have to do with our relationship to God? My personal experiences suggest that each person can learn to take account of what has been laid on their hearts. We would do well to pull back from what the world expects of us, such as the constant pressure to increase sales or the need to meet the expectations of others. We ought to seek out experiences of solitude and consider the fruit this labor might bear.

Faith paves a way in our lives toward change and flexibility; such attributes are necessary for experiencing fullness of life. The fact that we come to possess such trust is itself a way by which God leads us, in sharp contrast to the expectation that God must govern our every move. We might compare this to the experience of parents who engage their children in conversation as they grow. The children assume increasingly more responsibility while the parents offer them support and continually have their best interests in mind.

God is not like a father or mother who must make every decision for their infant children. God takes us seriously, honoring our freedom and upholding our responsibility.

Fortunately, we are able to recognize a sense of God's accompaniment when we find ourselves facing important life questions. Many people come to understand their work as a genuine calling and experience a profound sense of happiness when they discover their place in life. While we may not always understand where we are going, we know we must follow God's leading and are grateful for the experience.

Sometimes when we stand at a fork in the road and ask God which way to go, we hear nothing. God takes our freedom seriously. Just as children learn responsibility from parents who allow them to make their own decisions, we must grow in faith by cultivating spiritual maturity.

At certain times a parent must take their child by the hand and say clearly, "This is the way." Walking with God is relatively easy when we hear a clear word from him. In such times, we don't need to think very hard about what to do. But God often seems to wait at a distance as we make our decisions, allowing us to let our earlier experiences of him influence our future decisions.

In matters of faith we often behave in ways that are quite childish. When something goes wrong, we immediately hold God accountable and conclude that he doesn't take good enough care of us, as if it were God's responsibility to sort out all of our problems.

Of course it's wonderful when God says something to me and I pay attention, but relinquishing our infantilism in order to assume full responsibility for ourselves suggests that we have progressed to a more mature faith. While it is crucial to cultivate this maturity in our lives, we can't expect it to happen automatically. First and foremost, we must journey with God.

In my life I've come to treasure the experience of sensing God's presence and hearing a word in a given situation. Many of us have forgotten or never known this experience because the practice of attention is no longer taught. How does God speak to us? Some might ask whether God speaks at all.

Despite my sympathies, I find myself skeptical toward those who always seem to know, concretely and in great detail, exactly how God is speaking to them. I don't think we can be quite so certain. However, I'm convinced that my encounter with the South Seas missionary Pierre Chanel, whom I met through the pamphlet I found in the attic, was a concrete example of God's guidance. According to worldly standards, he was a man who experienced little success in his life. He was weak, which is perhaps why I could identify with him. As a missionary he journeyed to a South Seas island but was expelled by a chief whose son wanted to be baptized. The pamphlet told the story of what Chanel had to endure, such as eating worms and constantly traveling far from home. He finally lost all contact with his family and friends, yet to his mind, his experience continued to be worthwhile.

One lesson became clear to me: God brings success in his own time. Pierre Chanel experienced nothing we would call a measurable success in his work as a missionary. The only people he baptized were near death. We should not become discouraged when we don't immediately see the fruit of our work because we can trust that God will guide everything according to his own schedule.

Our life in modern society is structured very differently. We want to see success so that we can show it to others, but there is great relief in trusting that my work might have an effect— perhaps in the heart of another—even when I don't see anything happening. What I do can have meaning even though the results lie beyond my determination and surpass the domain of my responsibility. I can seek to act responsibly precisely because I do not have the freedom to do whatever I want; the question of my actions is not purely an arbitrary matter. I know that when I act, God is present and will bring things to pass in his own way and time.

It's the same with prayer. Trust is the precondition when you pray for God to watch over your children at school. While God's presence won't keep particular things from happening, he will encourage you to trust that your children must not face life alone.

Surprisingly Different

I can feel how trust unburdens my life. I never suffer from the pressure to succeed. I have my worries and needs like everyone else, but I also can say, "God, I have you, too!"

The pressure to succeed is pervasive in our society. In this regard, I am privileged as a monk, though I also face responsibilities. I can't simply step out of the world whenever I please. I'm now seventy years old and am continually asked: "What will you do when you're seventy-two? Will you stand for reelection as Abbot Primate?" I'd love to experience more quiet in my life, but this can't be the guiding motivation for making a decision. What is it that lies behind this desire for solitude?

It could be a matter of comfort. As Benedict reminds us, "Idleness is the enemy of the soul" (RB 48.1). Pope Emeritus Benedict XVI is an example of a person who undertook an enormous responsibility at an advanced age (he was born in 1927). The exhilarating sense of purpose we find in our lives can be part of our experience to the very end.

The death of Pope John Paul II was rich with blessing and exerted a powerful influence on me and many others, though in the pope's later years I heard critical voices say, "Get this fragile old man off the television screen; we can't bear looking at him!"

Believers and nonbelievers alike found themselves fascinated by the manner in which this man embodied his fragility and emanated a great dignity—this from the man whose public profile had once seemed indestructible. He knew that his value had nothing to do with how he looked to others; his appearance did not affect his ability to impact others in the last years of his life. He knew his worth was rooted in the inner core of the life God had given him. I am sure many people were influenced by his example.

Allow me to offer a story. Amid the celebrations that marked Pope John Paul II's funeral service, then-Cardinal Ratzinger halted President George W. Bush's Secret Service team from initiating their plan to vacate the church so that the President could pay his respects to the deceased pope alone. The crowd waiting formed a line more than two miles long that stretched almost all the way to the Piazza Venezia. As the most senior prelate in charge of these ceremonies during the vacancy of the papal see, Cardinal Ratzinger refused this request, telling the President's handlers, "We'll wait for you at a back entrance and the President can pray there, but you should not expect us to force all these people to leave during that time."

The capacity to oppose the pressure of political correctness exemplifies a way of thinking and acting that is based on listening to the heart.

God speaks to us today. While some might hope for a clear pronouncement in their lives, I suggest we don't wait for a voice from above before we act!

I will not rule out the possibility that God can speak perceptibly to us. Many younger people seem much more open to this prospect than those of my critical generation. That said, hearing the voice of God is rare. I did recently hear, however, a story a man told in regard to his girlfriend, a woman whose pragmatic worldview he valued highly. She told him that she once heard the voice of God speaking directly and audibly to her. According to my acquaintance, this woman had no tendency toward religious fanaticism. What would happen if there were more people like her who experienced such things and shared the experience with others?

I'm convinced that the world would look quite different. If you wish to experience God's voice, I encourage you to take God's presence in your life more seriously by becoming ever more mindful. In order to hear God, we must become quiet. God usually transmits over a quiet radio frequency.

In retrospect, we often discover that God has spoken at a particular time in our lives. When I look back, I begin to recognize the red thread, but to anticipate it by looking forward, as it were, is not so easy. For example, I currently find myself looking for a cellarer (an administrator) and can't find anyone fit for the job. Perhaps I need a different solution; perhaps my search has been misguided. Maybe I don't need a monk; maybe I need someone with special training for the job, someone who brings different gifts and experiences.

Prayer is almost always helpful in such situations. Many people feel they can't burden God with the little things in their lives. But why not? In the Bible we read that God counts the hairs on our head (see Matt. 10:30); from this we can assume that such a God is concerned with all the details in our lives.

God can speak to us through those we trust. Let's say that I have financial worries; my situation is not progressing as I'd hoped. It would be a great mistake to seek answers and solutions by myself. When I bring others into conversation with my questions, I always seem to arrive at a saving idea.

Last year, we found that we had to replace all 416 windows in San Anselmo, our university and the place of my current residence. We faced the unavoidable question: "Where are we to find the vast sum necessary for such a renovation, which is estimated to exceed several million dollars?" We could have delegated the cost to other monasteries in our order, asking them to contribute to the necessary improvement by paying for one or two of the window replacements. But many of them don't have even this kind of money. Another brother came up with an excellent solution that would help us stay solvent: "Notker, next year is your seventieth birthday, and many of your friends will be asking what they can give you. If they contributed to a fund designated for this purpose, this could surely help!"

I don't beg gladly for myself, but this was not for me. The gifts we received added up to almost a quarter of the entire amount needed! On the strength of these offerings, we were able to imagine completing the project. The situation reminded me that God doesn't speak to me alone; my life is inseparably interwoven into the tapestry we make together. St. Benedict says that in the case of crucial questions, the abbot should gather "the whole community together" and ask for advice (RB 3.1). By way of emphasis, he adds this explanation: "The reason why we have said *all* should be called for counsel is that the Lord often reveals what is better to the younger"—a counterintuitive claim, since we often assume that those with less experience don't have much to offer (RB 3.3, emphasis added). The younger monks might bring a fresh and more expansive perspective that helps us make the right decision in a given situation.

Listening to God can mean speaking with others whom we trust about situations we face in life. God often speaks to us through those who have open ears and hearts for him. If someone makes an unexpected suggestion in the process of such a decision, we would do well to suspend our spontaneous defensiveness and open ourselves to the possibility that such a solution might be from God. It is my fundamental belief that the future of San Anselmo does not depend on Abbot Primate Notker. It includes him, but not him alone.

This realization is a relief but also a provocation in terms of how our economy generally works. Imagine for a moment that you could live into the realization that the future of your company, or the future of your children, does not depend entirely on you. You would certainly feel unburdened. Try saying, quite simply, "Lord, I'm ready to employ my energies, fully and completely, with the awareness that everything does not depend solely on me."

Sticking Points and Stumbling Blocks

Many things can hinder us from recognizing God's message: everyday worries, stress in the workplace, the desire to accumulate, ambition, pressure from sales goals, fear of tests—the list goes on. Does God even have a chance to make himself heard? Do I let myself be so overwhelmed by my many activities and worries that there's no way to hear him? Amid such pressures, do I have any chance to be free and to listen? How much power do I give others in my life? It is clear that many people in our society face mounting pressures from many directions.

The question of power has its foundation in the fears we have about our identity. Who am I, after all? What do I have to say? We often feel as if we will lose something when we expose our struggles to others, inviting them into our decision-making processes. We fear losing our independence and often assume that relinquishing control means letting others decide what we should do.

These questions strike at the very core of our search for the meaning of identity: Do I exist only insofar as others give meaning to my life? Do the purpose of my life and my experience of who I am lie in the tasks I take upon myself? The question of identity is important, if not *the* deciding question we face.

Who am I? I am someone because I am a person made by God. This truth follows me from the beginning of my life to its end. Every person surrounding me is a creature of God, and we are called into community to live for each other and with each other. We are not

*alone. Faith can shape a healthy self-awareness within us. I am
someone, but I am not everything!*

As Westerners, we have been shaped by a tradition of
individualism and egocentrism. The example offered by the Chinese
is quite different. For them, the collective occupies the central place
of importance; the individual is not nearly so central. In Buddhist
cultures, the goal of life is the total immersion of the human person
in the life-flow of the cosmos. For a Buddhist, the Western idea of
self-actualization is not a goal worthy of our energies. Buddhist
teaching points to the importance of completely relinquishing the
sense of "I" that otherwise dominates our lives.

Christian teaching tells us that God created all people as
individual persons. My identity and the purpose of my life are
realized when my particular nature fully unfolds and becomes
part of the world I inhabit.

Everything that God has created within me is a component of
the unique person I am meant to become. Fear and egocentricity
stand in the way of our development, influencing our choices
and pressing us to separate ourselves from God in order to make
room for self-development and independence. In essence, we are
trying to make ourselves *like* God rather than living *with* God
and letting ourselves be led *by* God.

Considering Important Things Important and Unimportant Ones Unimportant

St. Benedict gives his monks sober and sobering advice when he
writes, "Day by day remind yourself that you are going to die"
(RB 4.47). He is not referring here to a longing for death or even
a fear of death but rather to a question of value: In the face of
death, what holds real importance? What remains valuable?

Our money won't go with us, and it may well be that our heirs will argue about who gets what. In some cases, such quarrels break families apart entirely. Names and titles are inscribed on our gravestones, and we molder in the ground below. Benedict's invitation is not meant to incite within us a fear of death; it calls us to recognize that the fact of our own death can relativize the things we often find ourselves chasing after. Keeping death before our eyes frees us.

Ultimately, we all know that death could be imminent and that sooner or later we must face it. When we do, we come to see that we are driven by many false ambitions and goals.

From time to time, we ought to step out of our lives. I don't mean we should go somewhere but rather that we try to find an inner distance from the things that drive us so that we can see more clearly the deeper connections that sustain us. Having done so, we can stand deliberately before God and ask:

"What would happen if I died tomorrow?" Rather than allowing ourselves to be defined by the expectations of others, we could define ourselves by God's love. Daily reminding ourselves that we are mortal might help us emphasize what is most truly important.

What counsel would you give friends who recognized that the reality of their lives collided what they found to be most important—if, for example, the pressures of work left them with little time for their children or their marriage? I'd advise them to take into account how they might arrange their lives differently, even if this meant finding a different job. If they realize that their way of life is not commensurate with how they would live in the face of death, a mature faith would help them trust God to guide their decisions.

Complete renunciation is usually not the best path to take because it avoids the task of facing and solving our problems.

Problems confront us no matter what shape our lives take. We must learn to live with challenges in a way that does not succumb to the illusion of an ideal form of life waiting beyond them. In Plato's *Republic* the question is raised whether the idea of a perfect state can ever be realized, and the answer is simple: no.

Young people often maintain an idealistic attitude that leads them to hope and work for justice, greater equality, and stronger solidarity with the vulnerable in our world. Eventually, they discover that life is not ideal and that they must grapple with compromise. The only way to experience the ideal is to stand outside the world as it is. But we live our lives in the world. While the ideal of the monastery might include the desire to escape from the world, the monk quickly finds himself caught up again in its realities.

Journeying with God and allowing ourselves to be redeemed means relinquishing false expectations and accepting the imperfect. When we can accept that every aspect of our lives cannot be perfect, our unrelenting need for control will finally abate.

The same holds true for our interactions with people we find difficult to accept. In facing this challenge I find myself saying: "God, you are the one who made this person, and you accept him. I am encouraged to do the same."

I had a good laugh when I heard a story from one of our students about an unbearable professor at the university who was extremely unfriendly and gave the students impossibly difficult assignments. One day he exceeded the allotted time for his lecture and gave the students a reading assignment to complete before the next class. An audible grumble could be heard from the four hundred students who filled the lecture hall, to which the professor responded: "What do you want, then? I'm not agreeable to you—is that it? You have it easy! You only have to endure me for one and a half hours each week. I have to face myself the rest of the time!"

This is a way of saying yes to our own imperfection. Occasionally, we would do well to admit our inadequacy, perhaps saying to ourselves: "Well that was certainly a stupid thing I did!" Taking such an attitude can help us say yes in the midst of the limitations of the world—which, after all, isn't heaven.

Who Determines My Worth?

How can we convey this approach to faith and life to children? Children can sometimes be quite cruel. At some schools, the expectation to wear designer clothing can be intense, as well as the pressure to be athletic and strong. Such things establish recognition and acceptance. How can we impart to our children the relative unimportance of such things so that they know they are loved, even if someone at school tells them they're fat or weak?

Of course, we also need to consider how to handle the children who are taunting others. While children certainly need to know that they are accepted unconditionally, parents are responsible for setting proper expectations. Children need to be reminded that such actions and attitudes are both unhelpful and unkind.

I recently watched a television program dealing with unemployed youth. The proprietress of a pet shop hired a young man for the day, only to discover that his manner of treating customers was appalling. He was unfriendly, rude, careless, and neglectful in tidying up the store. At the end of the day, the owner confronted him with his behavior: "How could I possibly hire you here? You drive away my customers. What earnings would I have left to pay you?" I don't know if the young man understood her warning because the show moved on.

Confrontation is sometimes necessary in order for young people to learn that they won't simply be handed things in life. When we desire something, we must learn to wait for it and invest ourselves in order to attain it; no one can guarantee that we will necessarily receive what we want. Growing up means coming to recognize that not everything we want exists, and what does exist won't necessarily come in the moment that we want it. In the years following the turbulent changes that began in 1968, we called this "frustration tolerance." Each of us must learn this skill. For children, this might simply entail finishing homework before going out to play.

Growing into adulthood means overcoming childish behavior and attitudes. As long as we chase blindly after what we think we must have we'll find ourselves missing our destiny and living under constant pressure.

If we understand that we probably won't get what we want most of the time, we can better adjust our desires and clarify whether such things are truly necessary for our happiness.

What expectations and demands do we bring to life? Does everything need to be bigger or more luxurious? This often seems to be the case with cars, though a large proportion of the world's population will never own one.

We need to teach our children this fundamental lesson so that they can make their way through life with far less ballast than might seem necessary. Above all, children need time. Many issues, questions, and problems need to be discussed with them. Consider the example of designer clothing: "What does it mean to wear the same shoes and clothing as everyone else? When you do, you lose the chance to express your individuality and become simply a face in the crowd."

A child might respond, "But others look down on me if I don't play by the same rules." Each of us must come to understand that our worth is not determined by what others say and think. Those who don't learn this early in life might never be able to extricate themselves from dependence on the expectations of others. When the opportunity presents itself to speak openly about such things with your children, take advantage of this important chance to share the truth with them. It's crucial that they understand: if you become a person who only follows the crowd, your life will be driven by others. You might be recognized, but the pressure will never end. When you do something in order to be recognized by others, your life will be unhappy because you will always be dependent on the opinions of others. You will have no real freedom because they will determine your sense of worth.

We shouldn't make this a constant topic of conversation; to do so might work against the message we wish to convey. As parents we can often sense the times when what we say can be heard.

When I decided to become a missionary and a Benedictine, I faced the disturbing question of what people would say about me. My teacher at school told us to first complete school and then turn our attention to decisions about the future, but for me, the matter was utterly clear: I already knew what my decision would be. This is what I want, I said to myself; I've set my mind to do it.

Over the course of my life I've learned to guard against yielding to the attitudes of others, and this has helped me avoid being captive to their expectations. I'm grateful to have learned this lesson.

Parents must be wary of being too critical in the way they guide their children, particularly during the years of adolescence when such an approach can lead to real difficulties. Yes, children need limits, but we must always find ways to give them freedom to experience life for themselves. Sometimes they need to be able to let loose. When a young person says, "I want to do some exploring, to try things out for myself"—well, why not?

Our youth can only grow into maturity through such experimentation. Parents can serve as guardrails, guiding their children away from serious falls, but young people must be allowed to make their way on their own.

Isn't our journey of faith similar? The stages of development children move through are not unlike those that we as adults must experience.

As Jesus says in the Gospel of Matthew: "Truly I tell you, unless you change and become like children, you will never enter the kingdom of heaven" (Matt. 18:3). It's a matter of holding onto the childlike freshness and spontaneity toward life—the freedom from anxiety children naturally possess—which is very different from a childishness that declares, "I'm going to jump from the steeple because God will protect me."

One of my monastic brothers, now long deceased, once told me how he wanted to test his faith as a young monk. He went out to the pond by the monastery and tried to walk across the water; naturally, he did not succeed. Soaking wet, he returned to the monastery, leaving a trail of water behind him. As a punishment he was required to eat "dirt soup," a form of discipline that used to be applied in monasteries. He had to kneel on the floor and spoon soup from a bowl that was at eye-level on the table.

In their earliest years, children feel protected by their parents. Their journey into adolescence is a necessary phase of separation that helps them begin to form their own identity as they move into adulthood and discover who they are. In terms of faith, we can only hope that they, like us, have the freedom to make their own discoveries. Spiritual development moves in stages—periods of time when we are able to find ourselves by exploring questions of faith naturally, but within certain limits. We certainly should not believe in just any fairy tale we hear.

When we journey on this path, our experiences will be akin to those of a child. First we will trust competent companions—reliable people who will guard and guide us—but we will need to find the courage to move beyond them in order to face our doubts honestly. This is entirely normal. Eventually, an inner certainty will guide us on our way.

Maturing in Faith

It should be said that the journey of faith is not a matter of course. We must grow in our faith, and this can be a demanding process. Mother Teresa of Calcutta was always known as a woman of great faith. Only after her letters and journals were published posthumously did we discover that her remarkable work on behalf of the poor was accompanied by a profound struggle of faith. Again and again she found herself plagued with doubt. John of the Cross, the great sixteenth-century Carmelite reformer, spoke in his own time of the "spiritual darkness" Mother Teresa faced throughout her life. He came to understand that we must experience the "dark night of the soul," as he put it, in order to be purged and refined.

While she is often lavished with effusive praise, Jesus's mother traversed this same path. The visitation of the angel was certainly unsettling, and the story reminds us that she was unprepared to simply embrace what she was told without question. Only after her questions were answered did she speak her yes and open herself completely to God.

Many Christians, particularly Protestants, experience significant resistance to the Catholic veneration of Mary. Yet as we probe more carefully into her story, we find how utterly human she is.

She carried Jesus for nine months under her heart and faced all the stresses of pregnancy. As part of her accepted calling, she was led to encounter her pregnant cousin Elizabeth. This meeting has been portrayed many times, with great sensitivity, in the church's art. It offers a visual image of the text recounted in Luke's Gospel, especially these words: "Let it be with me according to your word" (Lk. 1:38). Because of her capacity to trust, Mary's leap into the unknown unburdened her so that she could live God's word for her life.

Each of us must learn to take such responsibility for our own lives. When we learn to say yes to the quiet stirrings of God, we come to know that we don't stand alone and are part of a larger plan. This is a great encouragement, even if the situations we face remain complicated and difficult.

In the ongoing journey of her life, Mary had much more to learn, which meant she also had to endure suffering, an experience that must have been unforeseeable earlier in her life. Living by faith is a profound experience, but it won't necessarily be comfortable.

"Let it be with me according to your word." Those who can speak these words for themselves will be able to speak their own yes to God's way in their life, trusting that he accompanies them and that things will be as they should. When we allow our lives to be shaped by trust, what follows is, at the very least, fascinating.

Learning to accept imperfection in our lives is a freeing experience. Finding our way in the face of opposition is challenging, and being misunderstood can be a demanding learning process. When we are young, we seem better able to accept what comes our way. In my own call to monastic life, youthful idealism certainly played a role. Now that I'm older, I find myself more hesitant and cautious than I once was, even as I continue to mature along the way.

Christian faith offers one of the best approaches to life. Its moral formation develops depth of character and shapes our will; faith gives us the inner freedom to act and to grow.

When we read the Bible carefully, we understand that Christianity does not promise a triumphant, problem-free future. Throughout history, Christians have been persecuted; they continue to be persecuted today. And yet Christians also want to live in freedom, to be accepted by others.

It may be that, after suppressing and persecuting others in previous centuries, we must now experience persecution. The history of Christianity continues to be a complicated back-and-forth story, distinguished by its failures as well as the remarkable people who lived it. It is unlikely that the future of the church will reside in the West; its influence in Western society continues to diminish.

Many among us worry about the church's diminished importance. But ultimately the problem of dwindling attendance or the matter of the church's standing in society is not important.

The importance of the church consists in its expression of God's love and the authenticity with which it conveys God's embrace of humanity.

The great challenge facing the church is the experience of and witness to this love. The faith of the church, as a whole, lies in the process of maturity; in order to grow spiritually, she needs to be purified again and again.

Love Is the Way

The mediation of God's love belongs at the center of every person's life, as well as at the heart of Christian and ecclesial action. God's love, as expressed in the written and spoken word, depends on deeds devoted to the service of others. As mentioned earlier, the life of Mother Teresa offers a vivid example.

An acquaintance of mine told me about his trip to India some years ago. He had been invited by a Christian organization committed to working with children. In describing his experience with the group, he said:

> *You could really feel the power of love in their work with the children. Day after day the workers went to the worst slums in the city; I went with them and was profoundly moved by the experience. The driving motivation for their work was their love of others, a love shaped by their faith. I've never in my life seen anyone pray with such complete devotion as these children did when they gathered for worship. At the conclusion of the service, three girls who were ten or eleven years old came to me to ask if there was anything troubling me—so that they might pray for me. Who, in Germany, would ever approach another after worship to ask, "Is there anything in your life that we could pray for?" Hardly anyone. But there I experienced faith alive in works of love for others. Faith was palpable in this love, in prayer for others, and in such loving forms of accompaniment.*

Faith matures when it helps us live out of a fuller experience of love through the beauty and power of community. This example helps me to imagine the kind of expansive heaven we might live beneath!

One evening a man sent me an e-mail; half an hour later he wrote and sent me another. He and his wife were experiencing great difficulties. He didn't expect me to solve his problems but simply asked me to pray for him. His request was an honest one, and I assured him that I would entrust him to God's guidance.

We are all invited to find our own path of faith, one that opens us to greater love. How deeply do I open myself in order to discern where God's way for my life is leading? How prepared am I to give myself, in love, to others and to creation?

Our hearts grow larger, or—to recall the words of St. Benedict—they widen when we journey in God's ways. Not only will those who practice selfless love be led to others, but they will also be happy.

Permitting Doubt

We face doubts in our lives that we seldom speak about but that we cannot evade. How do we deal with doubt?

Anyone devoted to the Christian faith will sooner or later face doubts. When I hear certain sermons, I find myself asking, "Does he really believe what he is saying?" Doubts aren't forbidden. They can be quite helpful when they lead us to greater faith. The experience of doubt is part of belief, just as some measure of uncertainty belongs to love.

We can't directly see or feel God. Having said that, many realities exist between heaven and earth that we can't see—such as love, morality, and air. These things are as indemonstrable as God's existence. No one would doubt they are real, though some remain suspicious concerning telepathy.

There are certainly proofs for the existence of God, though these are not to be understood in terms of empirical science. If that were the case, we would speak of knowledge rather than faith. On what foundation, then, does faith rest?

Believing is a kind of trust. We trust Jesus and his witnesses, those who tell us about him. In Jesus, we encounter someone who shared his life with us while opening to us a reality that extends beyond this life. He often spoke of an entirely different truth regarding life, about a selfless form of love different from what we often experience in the world, and he exemplified these teachings when he died on a cross.

No one witnessed the actual Resurrection; this was no worldly event. But as a living person the resurrected Jesus encountered many people. This same Jesus lives and encounters us today in the loving ways we offer ourselves to one another, in worship, in music, and in the word he addresses to each of us. Jesus remains present, even though our encounter with him is not a direct one.

"Do not hold onto me," Jesus tells Mary Magdalene as she encounters the resurrected Lord in the garden (John 20:17). His followers wanted to touch and hold him, though he warned them that this was not possible because he had not yet ascended to his Father.

It's a matter of letting God be God. If God exists, then his immensity makes him impossible to grasp. To put it another way: if we could grasp God, he would be too small to be God.

We are often eager to determine what God should be like. Many people relativize Jesus, saying: "He was an impressive man, but the story about the Resurrection is likely exaggerated. A few of his friends probably took him out of the tomb. Why do Christians make so much fuss about the Resurrection? Why not just honor him as an extraordinary person?" We find conjectures like these among the earliest stories about Jesus.

Much that Jesus said during his life would be rendered invalid if he were not the Son of God and hadn't been resurrected. If that were the case, he would have died a meaningless death. As the apostle Paul says in his First Letter to the Corinthians: "If Christ has not been raised, your faith is futile and you are still in your sins. Then those also who have died in Christ have perished. If for this life only we have hoped in Christ, we are of all people most to be pitied" (1 Cor. 15:17–19).

The supernatural often transcends the limits of our imagination. Consider the stories throughout the Bible in which Jesus opens the eyes of those around him. Such experiences have the power to overcome every doubt for us as well.

In many situations, we trust what we hear or read from eyewitnesses, but as we see in Matthew's Gospel, many people doubted the Resurrection (Matt. 28:17). Even Jesus's disciples couldn't believe it at first; they were completely disconcerted with the news. Initially, they hid themselves behind closed doors out of fear, knowing they might be pursued. Thomas went so far as to say, "Unless I see the mark of the nails in his hands, and put my finger in the mark of the nails and my hand in his side, I will not believe" (John 20:25), whereupon Jesus came into the midst of the locked room where they were hiding, presented himself, and showed Thomas his wounds.

The Italian Baroque master Caravaggio painted this vivid scene in a powerful manner. He shows Thomas facing Jesus and touching him with his fingers while the other disciples stand by observing the encounter.

The Bible is not simply a report about such events. We can study these stories in order to ascertain the meaning between the lines. In this case, we know the door was closed, and yet suddenly

Jesus stood among the disciples. On another occasion, he ate with them by the sea. All of the reports concerning his appearances after the Resurrection convey a sense of mystery. Usually in these accounts the disciples initially don't recognize Jesus, even though they'd been with him for several years. He appears among them and just as suddenly disappears from their midst, as happened to the disciples walking toward Emmaus. He accompanied them for a stretch of the way, asking about what had just happened in Jerusalem, and yet they did not recognize him. It was only as they broke bread together that "their eyes were opened, and they recognized him; and he vanished from their sight. They said to each other, 'Were not our hearts burning within us while he was talking to us on the road, while he was opening the scriptures to us?'" (Lk. 24:31–32). He appeared in a different form from the one they had known; even his disciples were unable to recognize him.

If we act purely on the basis of what we can see, building only on the strength of our reason, we don't need to believe or trust anymore. All we have done is made ourselves and our natural capacities the ultimate measure of our faith.

An Enriching Diversity

Doubts can arise within us when we consider the ecumenical situation of our world today. It's understandable that each side perseveres in attempting to mediate the truth as they understand it in their particular church tradition. Yet despite the ecumenical dialogues conducted over the last several decades, the discrepancies between our accounts remain substantial. Theologians are divided even within their own faculties. One insists that the miracle stories must be interpreted according to the tenets of depth-psychology; another suggests that the resurrection of Christ must be understood in an exaggerated sense; and still others insist that it must be read literally. People who desire to renew their faith can be quickly confused by such diverse approaches and disagreements. This diversity is rendered even more complicated by the particular faith community in which we find ourselves as well as the nature of the congregation we grew up in. These origins shape us throughout life.

On the other hand, ecumenical discussions have made genuine progress, though the question of whether we will ever attain real unity is impossible to answer. Such an aspiration ultimately depends on the gift of God's Spirit, but it may be the case that we also have a false impression of what unity means. We often presume that unity is attained only by signing a contract that states we all believe the same thing—a process we witnessed in 1999 in the "Joint Declaration on the Doctrine of Justification" signed by the Lutheran World Federation and the Roman Catholic Church. But such a document hardly guarantees that everyone in these churches believes the same thing.

Already during the first centuries of Christian history, the period in which the New Testament took shape, one finds differences of belief and practice. After the Reformation of the sixteenth century, Catholicism came to stand alongside many other churches and denominations that make up Protestantism, including, eventually, evangelicals, those who make up the so-called "free churches," and more splinter groups than can be listed here. In South Africa alone, thousands of Christian groups have registered themselves as denominations. How are we to imagine a unification defined by official agreements of the sort mentioned above?

And yet all such groups are labeled "Christian" in wider society. Buddhists who wish to engage Christianity might be unsettled by the extent of this variety, but they will also come to see that all of these confessional groups, movements, and denominational institutions join in a common witness to Christ.

I recently studied the history of the Mennonites more closely and found myself deeply moved by their life and witness of faith. Though our theological views differ considerably, we are united on many points. In the midst of our diverse teachings and approaches, we share a common witness to Christ—a witness of love and particularly a commitment to peace. Since the sixteenth century, the Mennonites have supported the cause of peace. The conviction of their faith and their way of life often remind me of Pope John Paul II, who had strong pacifist leanings that led him to oppose the U.S.-led war in Iraq. In his denunciation of war, the pope held the view that "every war is a defeat for humanity."

Within the New Testament, we find a wide variety of theological views. My professor of New Testament, Otto Kuss, titled his introductory lecture, "Theologians and Theologies in the New Testament."

John the Evangelist wrote differently from Luke. John was intent on teaching his community about the presence of God in Jesus Christ and the ways in which Christ was embraced through the experience of his early followers. In contrast, Luke identifies with the poor and writes provocatively against the rich, while Matthew focuses on Jesus's preaching concerning the Christian life as it was lived in the congregation.

This is by no means unusual. As human beings, we emphasize and approach differently the things that move us depending on who we are. In relationships, diversity is also the rule; one partner approaches things in a romantic way, another with a pragmatic attitude. Those who are feeling-oriented experience love differently from rationally minded persons. In such matters, we can't say that one approach is better than another. We have varied takes on life, and each of us has to find our personal approach in order to discover and express the fullness of our being.

We should not be surprised that a man like Jesus was perceived in different ways by different people. We might even compare this to the books exploring Mozart's life that were published on the two hundredth anniversary of the composer's death. The many different portraits of this musical genius help us become more familiar with his life and work. While we know much more about Mozart than we do about Jesus, this knowledge has not diminished the variety of perspectives on Mozart's life.

Consequently, we should not see the diversity of approaches to Jesus as a threat to faith but as an affirmation that each of us can find our own point of view, discovering the approach that is best for us without devaluing the others. This attitude presumes we are seeking the truth, in which case the solutions that present themselves will also be varied. All of these processes belong to human experience.

I know a Catholic who once shared his understanding of Ash Wednesday with a friend who belonged to a free-church tradition and did not observe the day. Ash Wednesday marks the intentional beginning of Lent and is meant to shape the following forty days of penitential fasting. His explanation proved helpful to his friend, who commented that "it would genuinely enrich our faith if we were to observe such a time of fasting."

In such ways we begin to build bridges between differing expressions of faith. As I see it, theological differences and the variety of traditions should not give rise to doubt or sow the seeds of uncertainty.

In passages found in the New Testament, we hear Jesus speaking about people who cast out demons in his name but didn't belong to the circle of his disciples: "Do not stop [them]; for no one who does a deed of power in my name will be able soon afterward to speak evil of me. Whoever is not against us is for us. For truly

I tell you, whoever gives you a cup of water to drink because you bear the name of Christ will by no means lose the reward" (Mk. 9:39–41). Jesus's reply establishes the very foundation for ecumenical thinking!

When I read the New Testament, such as the letters of John or Paul, I find the earliest disagreements center on the question of what to do concerning false teaching. Another disputed question in these early sources concerns who Jesus truly was. Repeatedly found throughout these texts, this query remains a matter of great interest. Did he truly save us? If so, how? And what are the consequences for us?

Paul claimed that the weakness of the cross is our strength: "For Jews demand signs and Greeks desire wisdom, but we proclaim Christ crucified, a stumbling block to Jews and foolishness to Gentiles, but to those who are the called, both Jews and Greeks, Christ the power of God and the wisdom of God. For God's foolishness is wiser than human wisdom, and God's weakness is stronger than human strength" (1 Cor. 1:22–25).

Differences, doubts, and insecurities will always belong to our experience of faith. If we wish to have absolute certainty, we'll never believe; absolute certainty is not faith.

Desert Experiences

Faith is something different from knowledge, but this does not mean we know nothing. Rather, faith involves trusting in what we cannot absolutely know. This experience might be compared to our love for another person. In marriage, we go through difficult times, and doubts concerning our relationship arise in our minds. In spite of this, we know where we belong, and this deep knowledge reminds us that we can endure times of doubt without immediately walking away.

In spiritual writings, this experience is often described in terms of the desert. Believers face such times of doubt and stagnation just like the great mystics of the tradition did.

When we experience dark nights on our journey, we first need to acknowledge them and let them be. We must learn to trust that such nights are not a permanent condition; they will subside, and eventually we will see our lives in a different light. We should not presume or insist that our experience will be short-lived, and we ought to remember that we cannot grasp all things at all times. Humility is needed, and only humility can guide us on our way.

I was once hospitalized for a serious illness, and though I had been bedridden for more than four weeks, the prognosis on the day before Christmas was even worse. By Christmas Eve, I no longer cared whether God existed. I felt as if I'd fallen into an abyss; all that I could do was utter the short prayer, "*Kyrie eleison*, Lord, have mercy on me."

I was then able to see that as I fell into this deep chasm, a hand reached out to catch me. At the moment when I felt I'd lost all certainty and was prepared to accept whatever came—even this sense of nothingness—I had the distinct awareness that someone was holding onto me. My praying of the *Kyrie* eventually led to my voicing the Gloria on Christmas night. The experience of falling into a bottomless pit led to my sense of a hand grasping me as I fell. The poet Rainer Maria Rilke spoke of this in his poem "Autumn," published in *The Book of Images* (1906):

And yet there is One who breaks this fall
with the unending gentleness of his hands.

This experience transcends all doubt.

Being Carried in Our Suffering

We don't need to feel God near us all of the time. While this experience is always wonderful, it comes as a gift. Even Jesus faced times when he could not sense the presence of his Father, moments when he only knew God's distance. His shattering words from the cross, which we find in Psalm 22:1, come to mind: "My God, my God, why have you forsaken me?"

God caught Jesus in his fall to death. Our God is willing to descend with us into the deepest abyss and can empathize with our every need. This cry of dereliction—"Why have you forsaken me?"—means that Jesus had nothing whatsoever to hold onto for support. He could only trust that his Father would not abandon him to the dead.

When we find ourselves held fast in a dark night, even one that lasts weeks or months, we can still trust that God is with us. Such trust can strengthen our wavering faith until we are brought out again into the sunlight of a new day. Facing difficulty encourages us to cultivate deep roots.

When we once again experience the light, we are able to see more than this stubborn night. We realize not everything is dark and begin to look beyond our own circumstances and needs. We begin to notice the faith of others—how they face their struggles and allow good to flow through them.

In the case of beatification, the emergence of God's presence in the life of the person being considered for sainthood is of utmost importance. The person under examination has often accomplished extraordinary things that could not have been done without God's assistance.

Consider the example of the Benedictines and the ways in which they have helped others. If we were to eliminate from the history of Christianity everything done by Benedictine monks and other monastics, we would lose the structure of Western education as well as much of Latin literature during the Middle Ages. Monastic schools were instrumental in preserving the foundations of classical antiquity; scribes prayerfully copied thousands of manuscripts, making them available to readers for generations to come. The cultural landscape in the West would be entirely different without this great contribution; intellectual culture as we know it in our society would not exist.

From the start, the Benedictines were comprised of individuals pursuing their vocations in particular communities that had taken root where they lived. Monasteries had cultural significance; they were not simply focused on the spiritual lives of the brothers who joined them. Their cultural legacy became a worldwide legacy, an example of faith becoming manifest in history.

Love Made Visible

In his Letter to the Romans, the apostle Paul makes a claim that, when we reflect on it, we find to be true: "We know that all things work together for good for those who love God" (Rom. 8:28). "All things" includes experiences of suffering. When we open ourselves to God in difficult times, we are able to experience the ways in which God leads us to the good.

A single mother who aborted her child because she knew no other way forward but later experienced much suffering as a result of this decision, might come to say, "I don't want other young women to suffer as I did." She might devote her energies to founding an organization dedicated to this purpose, one that offers assistance and counsel for women. Through the demonstration of such love, other women would see that they are not alone and might be able to consider an option other than abortion. "We'll help you; we'll move forward together!" A great good might then come out of an experience of great suffering.

In the midst of our suffering, we often find ourselves capable of discovering things beyond the horizon of our familiar experiences. We learn things about ourselves that might otherwise have eluded us, such as being able to recognize a range of self-deceptions or perceive reality more truly as it is.

If we find ourselves developing a serious illness as a result of physical or mental burnout, it becomes important to shift our frame of reference. The question is not "How can I become healthy, as quickly as possible?" Instead, we should ask, "How can I live with this illness, and what can I learn from it?" When my father lost his job at the age of fifty-seven, my entire family supported him until he found another job. In times of suffering, knowing that we are not alone and don't need to do everything on our own is crucial.

Even Jesus knew loneliness. By the end of his life everyone had abandoned him, and even his disciples had turned away. In John's Gospel we read that Mary and John alone stood at the foot of the cross, together with two other women (see John 19:25–27). Jesus's sense of loneliness must have been extreme; he can certainly empathize with our suffering.

How do we face illness, suffering, or a job loss? When someone receives a terminal diagnosis and knows he is nearing the end of his life, he might make an assessment: "When I think about my life, who am I ultimately? What determines my value? Athleticism? Appearance? My career or achievements? Maybe by choosing to face this crisis with acceptance rather than resignation I can gain access to a deeper truth."

Pope John Paul II chose this path in his life. I know of people who rediscovered their faith because of his witness. When one becomes seriously ill, everything looks different. In his illness and death, the pope left us with an impressive example: he didn't conceal his fragility but gave witness to how a person's true worth can be found in the midst of weakness. In the last audience he gave, he appeared at the window of his rooms and lifted his hand in silent greeting because he could no longer speak.

In the end, it all comes down to realizing that God is our strength; for that reason, we are secure.

Suffering Is Part of Life

Many people despair of God's presence in the midst of a sudden tragedy in which innocent people suffer and die—whether it be children drowning in a tsunami or mountaineers falling to their death. In the face of such terrors, we often hear people say, "I can't believe in a God who allows such things to happen."

God is neither a nanny nor a bodyguard who stands on the sidelines and protects me from disaster or accident. To think so is utterly naïve.

In many ways, we seem to be incapable of improvement or change. In spite of tsunamis, fishermen rebuild their houses along the seashore, and when the next storm strikes we blame God again. But where else would they build their houses? They must live near the water. Our lives are in constant danger, in one way or another. We have been given no security or guarantee that our lives will be idyllic; such expectations produce a false image of happiness.

Natural disasters are simply part of our world. It is not incumbent on us to distinguish between those brought about by natural causes and those occasioned by human actions. Whether we are talking about climate change or climbers who fall to their death, accidents and unforeseeable events will transpire no matter how many precautions we take.

During my years as a student, I took the train from Germany through the Brenner Pass en route to Rome and was able to watch the great Brenner Bridge being built. Much of the work was done by welders fastened to ropes at staggering heights, and one day I read that three of them had fallen to their deaths. As I thought about this tragedy, Notker of St. Gallen came to mind. As a monk he observed workers building a bridge over a great chasm and recalled the liturgical text, "In the midst of life we are surrounded by death."

We come to know this truth as we face the realities of life.

Not every one of us will live to be ninety. Children continue to die in the world, and single mothers in desperate situations still abandon their children. We can't stop all such things from happening; nor can we know why they happen or what purpose they might serve. But we can try to ameliorate such situations by means of a mature faith, one that trusts in God in the face of tragedy.

I once knew a forty-two-year-old woman near death who called her husband and children to her bedside and told them: "Don't be sad. My life has brought me this far but no further. You've had me with you, and I've had you in my life; I've been able to give you this much of my life, which has been a great joy for me. Dear children, take care of your father as he cares for you. Study hard, be respectable, and find good careers. I'll accompany you from heaven."

She calmly said goodbye and took leave of her family, exemplifying a great maturity without hesitation or accusation. Happy are those who live by the guiding light of such faith.

"The LORD gave, and the LORD has taken away; blessed be the name of the LORD," Job said when he found himself facing report after report of terrible news (Job 1:21). His reaction wasn't simply a matter of resignation but rather a response that came from the strength of his faith. He knew he had no right to happiness and that everything in his life was in God's hands. For that reason he was secure. His hope was evident as he told his friends:

> For I know that my Redeemer lives,
>   and that at the last he will stand upon the earth;
> and after my skin has been thus destroyed,
>   then in my flesh I shall see God. (Job 19:25–26)

Faith offers the promise that everything will ultimately be renewed in God. This hardly means that we will, or must, receive an answer from God for every question in our lives.

We have to decide if we would rather ask questions about why a particular thing happens or try to help those who are hurting. God is always near in times of suffering, often offering consolation and presence in the form of other people. We, too, can become God's hands.

When we don't know what to do and are met by someone who offers to pray with us, we experience a great comfort. While comfort may not change the outward reality of the situation we are facing, such presence and encouragement can help us face suffering with the courage of faith.

We don't have the answers to many questions in life, and we don't need to. It seems to me that it is not necessary to have an answer for every question in order to be happy.

The Art of Letting Go

The capacity to let go is a great art because it allows us to let things simply be as they are. When we live into this truth, we come to realize that we don't have to accomplish everything that needs to be done.

The responsibility for the world is not mine; and it is not necessary for me to be able to explain everything.

In the statement that follows, St. Benedict describes the attributes needed for an abbot to properly exercise his office: "Excitable, anxious, extreme, obstinate, jealous or over suspicious he must not be" (RB 64.16).

When we succeed in putting such an excessive notion of responsibility behind us, many things in our lives will become easier. In our experience of suffering, we will no longer deplete our strength in a search for explanations. Instead, we will be free to concentrate on the path we must follow in order to be carried forward—though the journey may be difficult, and we may occasionally stumble.

When we do stumble, the strength of our faith can help us find the courage to let go of what we do not need to do and learn to trust the next step forward. If we don't rely on the wings of faith, we'll simply fall down and stay down.

Consider the example of those who can't swim. First they need to understand that learning to stay afloat calls for great self-confidence. Once they possess this confidence, they can venture into the water; without this inner drive to learn they'll not succeed.

Even if they find themselves swallowing water in the process, they will eventually realize their desire and become swimmers.

It can take great strength to avoid indifference in the face of suffering and doubt. The same is true concerning the reaction of shock and awe in countering suffering and death. It is enough to learn to take small steps, just as fledglings flap about ineffectively when they first leave the nest before they learn to fly. Consider the example of Jonathan Livingston Seagull in Richard Bach's well-known story. Practice is what strengthens our wings.

Our insecurity concerning how to make our first attempts at flight can prevent us from ever starting. But if we have the strength to try, we should take up our wings and jump from the nest! Only then will we discover the strength to defend ourselves against the cuckoo bird that tries to push us out.

What does this metaphor mean? During certain times in our lives we find ourselves inhibiting our own progress. Perhaps we've made the nest extremely comfortable and have become rather portly so that we no longer fit very well. That's when we know we've stayed too long and that widening the nest again isn't going to work.

When we find ourselves near burnout or experiencing our first heart attack, we can be certain that a cuckoo bird is trying to push us out of the nest. A cuckoo bird is someone who disrupts and threatens our life. His task is to throw us out of the security we've come to enjoy, prompting us to decide whether we're going to hit the ground or spread our wings and fly.

At times, the journey will be awkward. A sudden squall of wind might throw us off course. But just as a child becomes stronger through practice, each of us can develop the needed strength to stay on the path of faith.

PART

IV

faith that gives us wings

Overcoming Fear

The Christian faith enables us to trust in the knowledge that we are always journeying in the presence of God, or rather, that God is always journeying with us.

It is not incidental that the original title of this book was *Butterflies in My Stomach*. This metaphor is often used to describe the way we feel when we fall in love. And yes, I have fallen in love. Faith in God has a way of energizing and delighting us.

We are invited to thrilling experiences with God, just as when Peter climbed out of the boat and managed to walk on water, at least for a few steps. When fear suddenly overcame him, he cried out to Jesus in terror. And what did Jesus do? He reached out his hand, grasped Peter, and said, "You of little faith, why did you doubt?" (Matt. 14:31). With God behind us, we can give ourselves to every adventure that life offers.

When I took my first trip to China, and later to North Korea, many people thought I was crazy. "Aren't you afraid?" they asked. I wasn't. My faith gives me an unselfconscious outlook on the world that incorporates a childlike trust. It was no different when I decided to enter the monastery, even though I hardly had any idea what it would be like. My faith hasn't narrowed my life. Quite the contrary, it has enriched my life beyond what I could have imagined.

Those who have experienced the sense of being called by God find themselves experiencing sensations of joy and inner delight. A true vocation lures us away from the pursuit of comfort. When I am able to let go of my fear, I find that I can give myself to such a calling. In the process, I come to know myself far better than

I otherwise could have, and I gain so much more. Rather than circling around my own needs and desires, I discover someone else in the same way a lover does.

I imagine what it must have been like for Jesus to wander from place to place during his ministry. I once found myself sitting on a balcony beside the Sea of Galilee and sketched in my mind an image of Jesus walking along the beach with his first disciples. These were men who had abandoned their boats, left behind their nets, and turned from their fathers and brothers in order to follow him without hesitation. At some point they must have asked, in a state of some astonishment, "What have we done?"

But nearly all of them stayed the course. What Jesus promised must have been important enough to risk their entire lives. Since that time and in our own day, we know that innumerable others follow him on the same path.

How could these men abandon everything? Wasn't such an act irresponsible? If we are truthful, it seems a bit crazy.

But we also are invited to venture forth with Jesus, doing things that others would never dream of, things that would never occur to them. Unfortunately, they miss many experiences that are only possible for those who follow him!

The same is true with love. No one can predict what will happen when two people find themselves overcome with inner delight. The experience extends our horizons; no one knows what will happen as a result. Suddenly, everything seems possible.

The one who lives cautiously, always calculating the costs, might say, "I will only trust in myself." But neither love nor faith is a matter of calculation. Believers are able to say, "Let's see about it," entrusting their lives to a story that is more than two thousand years old.

How can we come closer to this story?

Experiencing Life Close to the Skin

I haven't spent much time in the Holy Land, but the little I've seen has made a great impression on me. I find myself reading the Gospels quite differently after seeing and experiencing some of the places mentioned in the Bible. Love for a place is much the same. I live in Italy, and many people love this land. They recognize the difference between baking a frozen pizza at home and enjoying a fresh pizza on a warm summer's evening, sitting outside on the veranda of a small Italian restaurant. The language, the fragrances, the sense of life, the entire atmosphere—all of it makes an incredible difference in our experience.

But Israel is more than this. We can imagine and, in a sense, experience what it might have been like for Jesus to walk along one path or another. In such moments, his humanity is no longer a historical abstraction. We can picture him pausing on a journey with his disciples, perhaps to explain the saying about needing to remove the log in their own eye before attending to the splinter in their brother's. He was their teacher, their rabbi, and their companion; as they walked together, he told them stories along the way.

I was particularly moved by my visit to Jerusalem. Experiencing the old city with its bustling life gave me a sense of what it must have been like in Jesus's day. I was fortunate to spend some time alone in the Church of the Holy Sepulcher, where I found myself remembering many of Jesus's words. All at once I realized that these words were first spoken here, in these places! I was deeply moved. When I found myself walking along the Via Dolorosa, the road along which Jesus carried the cross, I had the sense that these events could have happened only yesterday. The experience of such places awakens in me the reality of Jesus's life on earth.

Unfortunately, many of the sites from classical antiquity are built up to the extent that it is almost impossible to imagine what they were once like, though a few still convey an immediate sense of those ancient times. When I drive out of Rome along the Via Appia (one of the earliest Roman roads) and pass by the Church of the Domine Quo Vadis, I always think of Peter and how he wanted to walk away from this place so long ago.

I understand the feeling all too well. He must have felt very alone in Rome, even though he was surrounded by people. He recognized the possibility of martyrdom. Did he fear for his life? Or was he troubled by the question of what he was doing and what it all meant? Probably both.

According to the legend that recounts this story, Jesus met Peter as he fled from Rome, prompting Peter to ask, "*Quo vadis, Domine?*" ("Lord, where are you going?"). Jesus's answer to this question was simple: "I'm going to Rome to let myself be crucified again." In that moment, Peter knew what he had to do and returned to Rome where he was taken prisoner and eventually crucified. At the place of this encounter stands the Church of the Domine Quo Vadis.

Such an encounter with Jesus Christ must have been incredibly powerful for Peter to pursue his calling as he did.

We aren't speaking here of a feel-good faith. The stories recounted in the Bible concerning the disciples show us that Christian faith took shape in the midst of life. At times, the apostle Paul was deeply burdened by all that he had to do, yet in precisely such a situation we can see how faith offers us wings. As one of the great persecutors of Christians, Paul eventually became one of the most important and undaunted witnesses to the gospel of Jesus Christ. He came to experience a deep enthusiasm and love for Christ, "Woe to me if I do not proclaim the gospel!" he cried out to the Corinthians (1 Cor. 9:16). Paul perceived the message of Jesus as one of liberation: "For freedom Christ has set us free," he wrote, warning against becoming enslaved to the Law (Gal. 5:1). Addressing the pious of his day—strict Jewish believers who felt the need to keep the rules encoded in the Law to the letter, Paul insisted that faith alone is the most important thing. "For by grace you have been saved through faith" (Eph. 2:8).

I am motivated by the freedom and passion Paul came to have for Jesus (whose followers he had earlier persecuted), along with his capacity to stir enthusiasm in others and the way in which he encouraged them in their faith. He understood how to hold people's attention and bring them into his journey of faith. Many people, particularly those of an older generation, link feelings of fear with faith. But Paul and Peter must have evoked quite a different experience. What did they convey in their preaching? Love, hope, a sense of God's perspective, and the experience of total acceptance—their encounter with Christ was so gripping that others followed them, even to death. Passionate conviction is infectious.

This doesn't mean that Peter and Paul, two of the greatest apostles, were always of the same mind. Quite to the contrary, they found themselves at odds with each other. Paul courageously confronted Peter in Antioch in order to debate these important matters (Gal. 2:11–14).

The journey of faith encompasses every situation and circumstance. The Christian life is not simply a matter of courageously accepting whatever comes our way without criticism. Certain situations call us to confront each other, though in such circumstance we must be grounded in the truth and our desire to find the most faithful way forward, not the need to be right or the pursuit of power.

Faith as Inner Delight

How do I explain why my faith triggers an experience of inner delight, something like the feeling of having butterflies in my stomach?

Let me describe the experience of losing our sense of self-consciousness by again referring to the butterfly. A butterfly flutters happily about in a garden—first in one direction, then in another. It alights occasionally on a flower, sips some nectar, and then moves on in search of another strengthening drink. The Christian faith does not need to be unpleasantly serious, but neither is it superficial. Essentially, it grows out of an intimate freedom inside us.

While we shouldn't stop pondering things, not all of life is serious. Jesus savored life; so should we.

Too often we perceive faith as a matter of acting, or not acting, in a certain manner. In contrast, a butterfly knows what it needs to do in order to survive, but it also lets itself be carried about by the winds that come. If it were to struggle against them, then its strength would quickly diminish.

Some butterflies flitter about as they approach a blossom before pausing to drink of its nectar. Having discovered where the best nourishment for our lives can be found, we ought to share the same sense of eagerness. We will experience fulfillment if we allow ourselves to be carried by God's will and shaped through his strength.

The Transformation of the Caterpillar into a Butterfly

A butterfly does not simply appear, fully formed. It first takes the form of a caterpillar and then spins itself a cocoon. In certain phases of our life, faith grows almost imperceptibly, seeking ways to unfold and develop. Looking at a caterpillar, we cannot see what it will become; its development and transformation take time, though it will finally emerge as a butterfly of radiant beauty.

A caterpillar is confined to a narrow habitat, but when it becomes a butterfly the circumference of its life is vastly enlarged. Which do we wish to be, a caterpillar or a butterfly? Would we prefer to stay in the cocoon or break out of it in order to spread our wings and fly?

Faith can be like a protective cocoon within which we can develop into the person we are intended to be. As with a cocoon, we cannot know what sort of glory will eventually emerge.

The art lies in discerning the proper time to break out of the cocoon. If we emerge too early, our wings will not be fully formed, and we won't be able to extend them properly; if we wait too long, the flowers we need to live may have already bloomed and withered.

The laws of nature prevent the cocoon from opening too soon. Such laws can sustain us as well, though too often we abandon the rhythms of nature. Are we still capable of allowing things to ripen quietly so we can discern the proper time for them to emerge?

The wings of butterflies are particularly fascinating. We can't see them form, even though they are constantly taking shape within that humble shell. It is the same with us: only in the light of God's love can we develop into our fullest potential, revealing those qualities that we could not have possibly anticipated.

We can observe and admire the beauty and wonder of butterflies without tiring of the experience. In the missionary museum at our monastery of St. Ottilien, large display cases are filled with butterflies of myriad forms and colors from Africa and Latin America. The variety is extraordinary! In the same way, faith reveals our great diversity. Since we are made with varying colors and forms, each person believes a bit differently. This colorful variety is one of the most appealing elements of our faith.

Learning to Fly

Consider the birds. Imagine a fledgling that has not yet learned to fly. In its first attempts to leave the nest it may well fall, but if it does, the older birds will gather around and encourage it to try again. These experienced birds show their concern for the fledgling—feeding it, caring for it, and helping it practice until it can finally fly.

To become fully fledged in our faith means we must learn to master our lives through God's strength.

   Our perspective should be like that of an eagle quietly soaring the heights, allowing the updrafts to carry it into the sky.
   The Benedictine sister who preached a sermon marking the celebration of my seventieth birthday spoke about the eagle:

What is it that we wish for Abbot Notker today? The reading from Isaiah, which we just heard read to us, gives us an image for our wish:

Even youths will faint and be weary,
   and the young will fall exhausted;
but those who wait for the LORD shall renew their strength,
   they shall mount up with wings like eagles,
they shall run and not be weary,
   they shall walk and not faint. (Isa. 40:30–31)

Wings like eagles: this is a bold metaphor indeed. We all know how much Notker would love to lift himself up into the winds, and many think that if he can't take off, he must not be well. Nonetheless, this image of a proud and powerful eagle—the king of all the birds whose wingspan is immense and who builds its nest in the heights, a noble and rare bird that symbolizes power and victory—isn't this metaphor a bit too bold for what we wish to say on this occasion? Wings like eagles: what is it that we want to wish Abbot Notker by invoking such an image? Let's turn again to the Bible, which in this case describes the attributes of the eagle in a way that is consistent with scientific observations of the bird—and, in this sense, is a meaningful connection.

In the book of Deuteronomy, we learn that the eagle, in defending its nest and protecting its young, spreads out its wings, grasps the fledglings in the nest, and carries them atop its beating wings. Eagles build atop lofty cliffs, constructing their nests above deep chasms; we know this. How, then, are their fledglings able to learn to fly in such a precarious location? The adults take their young on their backs, and, flying from the nest, carry them out over the abyss—and then let them fall. As the fledgling tumbles through the air it seems to be lost, and then suddenly the older eagle who had been circling lazily above dives down and retrieves the young one on his wings, carrying it once again back to the heights. He continues to do this until the young eagle finally learns to fly on its own.

We wish our Abbot Primate, Notker, such courage for his work—to take it up, let it go, and begin it all again with sharp vision and the knowledge of the proper moment to act. We recognize in him the gift of spontaneity, the capacity to avail himself of what is new, and the wisdom to support sometimes unusual, uncomfortable, and yet daring initiatives among us. We know that he supports, with great commitment, those things he considers meaningful and important. May his trust in

*the Lord's working be renewed and strengthened day by day,
just as the eagle suddenly beats its wings—apparently without
great effort—and rises again into the heights.*

This strength and willingness to be carried is what I truly
experience, something that encourages me in my life and work.
My motto as an abbot reflects this: *Jubilate Deo*—"Praise God"!

*"Bless the Lord, O my soul, and do not forget all his benefits—
who forgives all your iniquity, who heals all your diseases, . . . who
satisfies you with good as long as you live so that your youth is
renewed like the eagle's" (Ps. 103:2–3, 5).*

I wish that all people had helpful companions by their side for
this exciting journey, just as I wish for myself the fellowship of
people who are devoted to pursuing the traces of God's presence
in their lives. When we fall like a young fledgling, not yet strong
enough in faith to make it on our own, the more mature can rush
to our side and gather us up again. The readiness to accompany
others until they are able to fly is an important pastoral
responsibility.

The question of being able, and wishing, to regard our faith
in God as the blueprint for our life is very personal. It's always a
risk. When we realize what we must let go of and the changes that
will draw us out of our familiar and comfortable way of life, fear
sometimes take hold. Yes, faith will bring changes to our lives,
though this happens first within us, in our deep inner life.

But when we alter our vantage point, we begin to realize that
this sort of relinquishment is not tragic. When one is considering
whether or not to enter a monastery, well-intentioned friends
often voice their concern with words of warning: "You'll no
longer be allowed to do what you want."

I would reply, "I don't need to do all those things." What appears to be denial can actually suggest a great gain that frees us of many desires and dependencies.

This is true not only for those in a monastery, but also for people in every walk of life. The freedom we experience in relinquishment widens our vision and expands our heart. We find ourselves developing a heightened capacity to perceive the traces of God's presence, and many things we once thought important no longer seem necessary. We find that we are able to be more loving toward ourselves and others because we realize that God has not called us to a life burdened by pressure and worry. We come to recognize what life is truly about.

Love, and Love Again

Faith is about trust and, above all, what it means to live in love. Love frees us, gifting us with the acceptance so many of us yearn to experience. Love makes us happy—whether we are speaking about God's love, the love we give to and receive from others, or our own ability to see with compassion. The wounds we experience—whether they be the pressure of expectations, our fear of being spurned, or anything else that burdens us in life—are all covered by the mantle of love. A loving way of seeing the other protects us from frustration, worries, and pressures.

The centrality of love is attested to in one of the most treasured of biblical passages, the great song of love found in the First Letter to the Corinthians:

If I speak in the tongues of mortals and of angels, but do not have love, I am a noisy gong or a clanging cymbal. And if I have prophetic powers, and understand all mysteries and all knowledge, and if I have all faith, so as to remove mountains, but do not have love, I am nothing. If I give away all my possessions, and if I hand over my body so that I may boast, but have not love, I gain nothing.

Love is patient; love is kind; love is not envious or boastful or arrogant or rude. It does not insist on its own way; it is not irritable or resentful; it does not rejoice in wrongdoing, but rejoices in the truth. It bears all things, believes all things, hopes all things, endures all things.

Love never ends. But as for prophecies, they will come to an end; as for tongues, they will cease; as for knowledge, it will come to an end. For we know only in part, and we prophesy only in part; but when the complete comes, the partial will come to an end. When I was a child, I spoke like a child, I thought like a child, I reasoned like a child; when I became an adult, I put an end to childish ways. For now we see in a mirror, dimly, but then we shall see face to face. Now I know only in part; then I will know fully, even as I have been fully known. And now faith, hope, and love abide, these three; and the greatest of these is love. (1 Cor. 13)

What particularly fascinates me in this passage are these words: "And if I have prophetic powers, and understand all mysteries and all knowledge, and if I have faith, so as to remove mountains, but do not have love, I am nothing." Everything that pious people might be able to accomplish would be nothing without love.

The opening verses of this text relate to *me*. Love first sets me free, helping me to free myself from myself. All things center on this truth.

In God we encounter an unqualified love.

To live in faith is a decision to live our lives in love, which means helping others by being present and concerned for them. In a word, viewing others with the compassionate eyes of God.

The passage from First Corinthians carries a great explosive force. It turns on its head our traditional image of piety. Piety alone has no value; it is worthless if it is not accompanied by selfless love. Many of us who spend considerable time in the church fail to see the beggar on the street corner and do not recognize our neighbor's needs. I'm sure that mothers who raise their children with love will enter heaven ahead of me. I have great respect for them. Only in the context of love am I ultimately able to live out my faith, and I must learn to live in love with intentionality. Sometimes we must change certain things in our lives in order to accomplish this, but not everyone must enter a monastery. Above all, the change begins with the way we view and relate to possessions. How often does ambition lurk behind the things we do? We can learn from mothers who live their lives for others.

And if I were intelligent enough to understand "all mysteries and all knowledge" my understanding would have no meaning until it was completed through love.

"If I speak in the tongues of mortals and of angels, but have not love . . ." I could be a remarkable preacher, but without love "I am a noisy gong or a clanging cymbal." A demanding word indeed!

We need to remind ourselves continually that without love, we "gain nothing." Be certain that the apostle Paul has deliberately emphasized the word "nothing"!

Only at this point does he turn to a description of love itself.

Love is patient; love is kind; love is not envious or boastful or arrogant or rude. It does not insist on its own way; it is not irritable or resentful; it does not rejoice in wrongdoing, but rejoices in the truth. It bears all things, believes all things, hopes all things, endures all things.

An impossible demand, many might say. So often we emphasize flawed values, saying, "It's impressive what they are able to undertake and accomplish!" While it can be remarkable to see how much some people do in their lives, accomplishments that are not shaped by love mean nothing.

For this reason, love is never separated from faith. In fact, faith develops and becomes real only through love: in this way faith is completed.

Faith can help us become a loving person or encourage us to become the loving person we once were. It frees us from the grip of false perceptions and expectations—our own as well as those others place upon us. It leads us to our true self and thereby to others.

Faith is not an accomplishment we recognize as the high point of our lives; it is the substance that gives our lives beauty and meaning.

Faith fills our existence with a sense of deep purpose. It allows us to feel a lightness of being because it enables us to throw off the unneeded and unhelpful ballast with which we try to fill the emptiness in our lives.

Those who have come to experience this lightness are able to lift themselves into the air. We must climb out of the nest like fledglings and dive off the cliffs like eagles, falling into the depths in order to discover the use of our wings. To recall the metaphor with which we began, we learn to be carried by our trust in God' love, like butterflies drifting on the winds.

Whether you feel like a butterfly or an eagle—whether you are a fledgling, a caterpillar, or a chrysalis held in the protective shell of a cocoon—let's fall and begin to fly! When we do, we will discover that we never fly alone.

About Paraclete Press

Who We Are

Paraclete Press is a publisher of books, recordings, and DVDs on Christian spirituality. Our publishing represents a full expression of Christian belief and practice—from Catholic to Evangelical, from Protestant to Orthodox.

We are the publishing arm of the Community of Jesus, an ecumenical monastic community in the Benedictine tradition. As such, we are uniquely positioned in the marketplace without connection to a large corporation and with informal relationships to many branches and denominations of faith.

What We Are Doing

Books Paraclete publishes books that show the richness and depth of what it means to be Christian. Although Benedictine spirituality is at the heart of all that we do, we publish books that reflect the Christian experience across many cultures, time periods, and houses of worship. We publish books that nourish the vibrant life of the church and its people—books about spiritual practice, formation, history, ideas, and customs.

We have several different series, including the best-selling Paraclete Essentials and Paraclete Giants series of classic texts in contemporary English; Voices from the Monastery—men and women monastics writing about living a spiritual life today; award-winning poetry; best-selling gift books for children on the occasions of baptism and first communion; and the Active Prayer Series that brings creativity and liveliness to any life of prayer.

Recordings From Gregorian chant to contemporary American choral works, our music recordings celebrate sacred choral music through the centuries. Paraclete distributes the recordings of the internationally acclaimed choir Gloriæ Dei Cantores, praised for their "rapt and fathomless spiritual intensity" by *American Record Guide,* and the Gloriæ Dei Cantores Schola, which specializes in the study and performance of Gregorian chant. Paraclete is also the exclusive North American distributor of the recordings of the Monastic Choir of St. Peter's Abbey in Solesmes, France, long considered to be a leading authority on Gregorian chant.

Videos Our videos offer spiritual help, healing, and biblical guidance for life issues: grief and loss, marriage, forgiveness, anger management, facing death, and spiritual formation.

Learn more about us at our website:
www.paracletepress.com,
or call us toll-free at 1-800-451-5006.

SCAN
TO
READ
MORE

You may also be interested in . . .

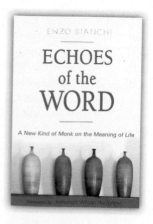
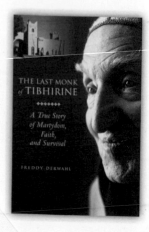